Competition Handgun Training

Warning:

Firearms are potentially dangerous and must be handled responsibly. The information contained in this training program is not meant to be used by a novice, or by someone who has not received proper instruction. The information in this book is intended for academic study only unless the reader complies with and ensures that they receive proper instruction on the use of as well as safety procedures required for firearm use. The author, Shooting-Performance, and any party associated with either assume no liability if injury, death, or unintended damage occurs during the use of this program, or from information contained in this book. If you do not wish to comply with safe firearm practices, please return this book for a full refund, and **do not read any further!**

Also by Mike Seeklander:

Your Competition Handgun Training Program

Your Defensive Handgun Training Program

Competition Handgun Training Drills

Competition Handgun Training Drills and Skills Volume 1 (DVD)

Competition Handgun Training Drills and Skills Volume 2 (DVD)

All available at www.shooting-performance.com

Copyright © 2013 by Mike Seeklander

ISBN-13: 978-1493722983

Printed in the United States of America

Published by Shooting-Performance

P.O. Box 2016

Owasso, Ok 74055

Direct inquiries and or order to the address above, or www.shooting-performance.com

All rights reserved. Except for use in a review, no portion of this book may be reproduced, stored in or introduced into a retrieval system, or transmitted in any form without the express written permission of the publisher. The scanning, uploading and distribution of this book through the Internet or any other means without the permission of the publisher is illegal and punishable by law. Please respect the author's rights and do not participate in any form of electronic piracy of copyrighted material.

Neither the author nor the publisher assumes any responsibility for the use or misuse of information contained in this book.

Welcome and Introduction:

Thank you for purchasing this logbook. This logbook is designed to be used in conjunction with (or by itself) my book "Your Competition Handgun Training Program", a training program designed for practical shooters (IDPA and IPSC/USPSA). This logbook will allow you to document and track your metrics (training, match, and other skills) and document your successes and learning points. The book has several sections, starting with some education and reminders about training, and followed by the logbook pages that will allow you to log all of your training sessions, as well as events that you compete in.

To order "Your Competition Handgun Training Program", please visit my website: www.shooting-performance.com

A bit about Shooting-Performance, my consulting/training company-

- I began Shooting-Performance (www.shooting-performance.com) as a free information sight where I could share my thoughts and lessons learned with whoever landed on the site. That evolved into some consulting, coaching, and some published material in the form of this logbook, and a couple other books (that are being finalized as I write this), as well as numerous articles. My original interest and passion lay not in teaching specific technique (as I believe it should always evolve), but in getting shooters from all walks of life to understand how to make their training more effective. Most of my students ask a common question, even after they have a good grasp of how to perform the techniques taught in a class, and that is: How should I train? My answer is often short due to time but in reality I understand and try to promote the fact that how you train will dictate how you perform, and proper design and execution of training sessions is critical.
- There is tons of useful information in the form of web pages, documents, and some video and you will also find a question form that will allow you to send me a question and get answers. Please visit my website, and drop me a line if you have a shooting comment, question, or revelation!

Remember, amateurs train until they get it right, professionals train until they can't get it wrong...AND they log their successes!

SECTION I

SIX PRINCIPLES OF AN EFFECTIVE TRAINING PROGRAM	7
SOME BASICS ABOUT DOCUMENTATION	11

CORRECT DESIGN AND PERFECT EXECUTION = PERFORMANCE ON DEMAND

SECTION II

GENERAL PLANNING FORMS	15
DRY FIRE TRAINING SESSION LOG PAGES	27
LIVE FIRE TRAINING SESSION LOG PAGES	131
MATCH/EVENT LOG PAGES	253
SKILLS TEST ONE AND TWO (TO TEST AND DOCUMENT YOUR METRICS)	
(THIS IS IN THE REAR OF THE BOOK FOR QUICKER REFERENCE)	267

Six Principles of an Effective Training Program

"Relentlessly pursue your preparation, like your life depended on it."

The Six Principles of effective training: In order for a training program to be effective, it must follow certain principles. Failure to contain or follow even one of these principles will render a program ineffective. Pay attention and validate your program by comparing it against these principles on a regular basis. Let's break each one down.

- ***Training sessions must be designed correctly.*** This is the first validation of your program. It could not be simpler, but this is often the area that I see wrong with most programs/drills that I have come across during my career. The learning goals must be thought out and defined and then applied throughout the drills that are used. Even programs developed with the best intent will be problematic if you don't pay attention to design. I will expand on this in the "Training Design Cycle" section. The two key areas you should validate in the design of your program are:
    - Skills developed must be applicable with the key factors desired (environment, gear, dynamics).
    - Skills developed must replicate the actual key skills needed. (This is an area that some really good athletes/operators argue about, because everyone has a slightly different idea about techniques and tactics.)
- ***Training repetitions must be executed perfectly.*** I will expand on this one in the "Training Design Cycle" section so I will be brief here. This principle is simple, and is a key component to success.
- ***Training sessions must be at regular intervals.*** In order to develop skill (purpose of training), the brain and neuromuscular system must be exposed to developmental sessions on a regular basis. How often is very much debated, and will generally depend on the goal, but across the board almost all of the experts agree that development must take place a minimum of two times or more every week during the initial learning phase, and then one time per week to maintain skill. (We will expand more on this later.)
- ***Training sessions must be documented.*** In order to reflect on the program's success, training programs must be documented. Key metrics should be written down for future reference, and you will use this data to modify the program as you go.
- ***Skills and abilities developed must be measured.*** Simply "feeling" that you are improving is a dead end road. Take the time to measure your skills on a regular basis. Someone once said that something that can be measured can be improved. Measure your skills or the skills of your group regularly to guide you through the program modification phase.

- ***Must be modified based on results (game day)***. A good training program MUST be modified. If not, results will stagnate and skills will remain in one place. Unless you desire this (not likely), you will need to reflect on your training logs and modify your program to continue your evolution.

The Design and Execution Cycle (see figure 1): How do the best shooters constantly push themselves to the next level? They constantly modify their training to meet their goals, and they constantly set the bar higher each time they accomplish a goal. Now that you understand what training design and execution are, I will attempt to describe the "Training Design and Execution Cycle" and offer what it will do for you. What is this cycle? To put it bluntly, it is the cycle that MUST be gone through to continue to evolve to the next level. Most people go through this cycle without even knowing it, but without understanding our training cannot possibly evolve. All too often I hear from someone who does not understand how to design their own training program, or that they must react to their failures (or successes) and constantly re-design their program in order to be successful.

Some Basics About Documentation

"Fail to document, and you will never see your failure"

Purpose of Documentation. Documentation of training sessions and game day is probably the single most important thing you can do to increase the effectiveness of your training program. I have made the huge error in failing to do this in the past and have regretted not having the ability to look back at my notes and use them to increase the effectiveness of my training program. One thing that really stands out is, other than my match finishes and some random times on the PACT timer I use to train, I really had no way of knowing if I was improving once I reached a certain skill level. I thought my training sessions were effective, but did I have the proof? I have since started logging all training sessions and matches just like I am outlining in this section and I have found this to be extremely valuable and usable information when I review it later.

Types of Documentation. When documenting your training sessions and events (game day), you will have a couple options. The first is good 'ole fashioned pen and paper and is the primary method we need to document. The second is video and/or audio documentation of your sessions. I STRONGLY recommend BOTH when you are documenting, because each has a different use when reviewing data and improving your training processes. If you are a trainer that trains large groups, I recommend that you issue and mandate training logs to all of your students. Make them document their training so they have a reference later on. In the Marine Corps, we had little logbooks issued in boot camp and we used them to log every range session we attended.

> *Written Logs.* Written training and event logs are the simplest and easiest way to document your training sessions. Your written logs should capture a lot of critical data. The logs in this book are pre-designed to make your job of documenting easy and fast. There are adequate logs in this book to capture all of your dry fire and live fire sessions if you are doing the 16-week program in my book "Your Competition Handgun Training Program", and then some extras to allow you to log your training for an entire season.
>
> *Video.* Video is the wave of the future. There is nothing comparable to it in terms of having true documentation of what you actually did during a drill or event. In your written documentation you can capture your metrics and how you felt during the performance of your drills, but you don't always get the whole picture. I can't tell you how many times I have seen myself on video and noticed something that I had no idea I was doing. I have also used video to show countless students small things that they are doing wrong, especially when they don't believe they are doing it. I use a tripod and a

small, cheap camera to capture my training session drills. If you are really cool, you can spend some money on a camera with a remote, but I have been told that these are hard to find these days (not sure why). This will allow you to set up the camera and then start and stop it with the remote. I set my camera up in a position so I can see as much as possible during the drill. I normally set my gear bag up near the camera so I can get my gun ready and prepare my magazines with ammunition, and then I start the camera and walk out to my shooting spot where I am going to do the drill. You will probably want to mark the spot you are shooting from (or set up a shooting box) so you know you will be centered in the video when you are doing your drill. I don't video my entire sessions, but I do video critical drills that I might be having trouble with.

Analysis of Documentation. O.K., so you are documenting like crazy with written and video logs. You're done with the hard part right? Not so fast. Now You have to use that information that was painstakingly recorded during training sessions and events. When you review your logs it is important you analyze them correctly, and in a certain order. I will break this down by timeline.

> *Post session review*. This review and analysis is done right after our session, or as soon after our session as possible. You should review your video first (normally you probably won't view the video on the range, but you can), because what you see may need to be logged into your session or event notes. If you see yourself doing something wrong on the video, enter it in your "need solution to" written log section. Now review all other notes, and take a moment to transfer key items to the next log you will use. You probably have your future session planned, but your notes from this session will affect some of the things you will work on during the next one. If you write down notes on your future log reminding you of some things you want to work on, this will make your next session more effective. Each training log should affect your next session, even if just to validate what you are doing (because it is working).

> *Pre session review*. This review will be done right before you begin your training session. Look at the last session notes, and also at what you carried over from your last session. You might look at some of your key metrics (times and points) from drills you did so you have some idea of where your metrics should be during this

session. Take a moment and glance at your goal statement so you know why you are going through all of this work! Extra motivation is always a good thing.

- ➤ ***Monthly review***. I like to take my training session notes out and lay them in order and look for trends on a monthly basis. This will only take a moment, but is really a great way to see if you have some good or bad trends happening. You will also be able to compare your metrics and hopefully see them improving across a month's time. Seeing improvement is a big key to your success! Look for gear and gun issues that seem to be recurring, and any other things that stand out when you look at a month's worth of data. Make sure to take a couple notes on your monthly review and what you found so you can plug that stuff into future sessions. I don't normally recommend changing your program with just one month's data.

Cycle or Yearly review. This data review is where you will look for trends that will influence your decision to change your training program. Once again lay all of your data out and take notes on good or bad trends, as well as your performance metrics. You should see some distinct improvement in them after you have been through a complete training cycle, and if not you will want to look hard at your drills and how you are training. No improvement can be a result of many different things, like poor drill design, lack of frequency (you're not training enough), lack of duration (you're not training long enough), etc. The notes from this review will be what you use to modify your program.

General Planning Forms

"Fail to plan, plan to fail"

Instructions: These planning forms are designed to allow you to plan your training year and also break down and roughly schedule your monthly training sessions. You will need to do this so that you when you begin your training plan you peak when you need to and don't burn yourself out. Some of you will have multiple events you will be training for and competing in and this makes it even more important to plan your year out and know what training sessions and drills you will be doing when. I have certain timeframes that I need to prepare myself for a major match, and it has taken me several years to figure this out. Your timeframes might be completely different than mine and this is something you will have to experiment with and log. Some of you will just train when you can for an event, and this is okay too, but it is still a good idea to plan your year, and even more important to develop your monthly matrix so you can plug all of your different training sessions into it and make sure it all fits. You will also begin to write down your goals in this section. Here are some guidelines for each form:

- **Yearly Training Plan.** A yearly training plan is a good idea if you have different phases of training you go through. It will help you structure your training into goal-oriented cycles, as well as plan better logistics. I mainly use one for competition type training, but it is a good idea for defensive training as well. Document any major training events, as well as specific cycles you might be focusing on. See the sample on page 22.
- **Monthly Training Matrix.** This is where you break down each month, so that you know exactly what you are going to do each week of the month, and general what days. It is a big help if you are integrating physical fitness (a must!), shooting sessions, dry fire sessions, and maybe combatives.
- **Goal Setting Worksheets.** This is where you will build your future. They are the most important part of the performance process. The goal setting worksheet should be a tool that you use to ensure your success.

Goal Setting Worksheet-

Instructions: This worksheet will guide allow you to set your goals and have them in your logbook for your weekly review. Instructions and a detailed explanation of the goal setting process can be found in my book "Your Competition Handgun Training Program", which I strongly recommend you purchasing if you have not already.

Competition Handgun Training Logbook

End Goal (written in first person, and should have a target date):

_____
_____
_____
_____
_____
_____

Performance Goals (these are the performance factors that will allow you to meet your end goal):

1. _____
   _____
2. _____
   _____
3. _____
   _____
4. _____
   _____
5. _____
   _____

Enabling Goals (these are the actually enabling actions that you will have to follow to develop the performance required in your performance goals). Simply copy your performance goals into the main section of this table, then write the actions required to meet those goals below them:

Performance Goal	Enabling Goals (Actions needed to accomplish your performance goals..be detailed!!)

1. **Scheduling:** Now take the enabling goals written above, and begin to plug them into the yearly, and monthly planning forms below, as well as your calendar if you have one that you use on your phone or computer. I recommend that you schedule your action like you would schedule an appointment for a job or someone else (like it is a formal date to do something).

2. **Print, Copy and Review:** Your goals MUST be reviewed regularly. Print them on a computer, or make copies of what you just developed and hang them in critical areas. Also, since you have your goals written in this logbook, make sure you read them at least weekly (beginning of the week is best).

Second End Goal Worksheet (if you have ore than two, email me printable goal setting form):

End Goal (written in first person, and should have a target date):

_____
_____
_____
_____
_____
_____

Performance Goals (these are the performance factors that will allow you to meet your end goal):

1. _____
   _____
2. _____
   _____
3. _____
   _____
4. _____
   _____
5. _____
   _____

Enabling Goals Simply copy your performance goals into the main section of this table, then write the actions required to meet those goals below them:

Performance Goal	Enabling Goals (Actions needed to accomplish your performance goals..be detailed!!)

Sample Yearly Training Plan

2010 Competitive Season				
Dates and events		**Key Dates Training Program Modules**		
Month	*Major Events/dates*	Live Fire	Dry Fire	Physical Fitness
January	Base fitness, general skills	01/02	01/02	Begin 12-week fitness program 01/02. Begin dry fire skill program 01/02.
February	USPSA skills Florida Open		02/18	Begin 12-week USPSA skills program 02/01.
March	USPSA skills			End 12-week fitness program, maintenance program. Begin 12-week USPSA program 03/01
April	USPSA skills	Single Stack Nationals	04/02	
May	Bianchi skills (NRA Action)	Bianchi Cup	05/15	
June				
July	Steel Challenge skills			Begin Steel challenge program
August	Steel Challenge skills	Steel Challenge	08/23	
September				Begin USPSA skills program 09/01
October				
November				End Season Review

Your Yearly Plan

_____Year/Season

MONTHS AND EVENTS		KEY DATES TO BEGIN TRAINING MODULES
Month	**Major Events/dates**	Notes. Example: Begin Live fire Training, Begin Dry Fire Training, Physical Fitness
January		
February		
March		
April		
May		
June		
July		
August		
September		
October		
November		
December		

Mike's Sample Monthly Training Matrix (this was one of my actual plans training for competitions)

Training Type	Frequency (How often)	Duration (length)	Days/Times (When)	Purpose/Notes:
Live Fire Practice *(may also be supplemented with .22 practice)*	3 times weekly	1.5 hours	Mon, Wed, Friday 0830-0930	Three separate sessions, each focusing on a certain area.
Dry Fire Practice *(may be supplemented with air soft practice)*	5 times weekly	15 minutes	Monday-Friday After 1800 (6 p.m.)	Per my dry fire training drills.
Mental Training *(MUST be integrated in all live and dry sessions!)*	3-5 times weekly	N/A	Active- Each practice Passive- Every night before bed	Passive visualization will be done on the upcoming performance. Active, every time I touch the gun.
Physical Fitness Training	3 times weekly	1-1.5 hours	Mon, Tue, Thurs, Fri 0600-0730	P90X modified program
Visual Training	2 times weekly	10 minutes	Wed and Sat	7 exercise program
Game Day *(this might be a match or anything else you are training for [the test])*	1 time monthly (minimum)	N/A	Monthly 4th Sunday (USSA IPSC match)	ALL matches should be treated the same. Never place more emphasis on one over another in your mind. "I need to shoot good because this is the big match" (Not good)

Your Monthly Training Matrix

Training Type	Frequency (How often)	Duration (length)	Days/Times (When)	Purpose/Notes:
Live Fire Practice (may also be supplemented with .22 practice)				
Dry Fire Practice (may be supplemented with air soft practice)				
Mental Training (MUST be integrated in all live and dry sessions)				
Physical Fitness Training				
Visual Training				
Game Day (this might be a match or anything else you are training for [the test])				

Mental Routine Worksheet:

1. **Focus Breath** (write what length your focus breath will be, and what actions if any that you will do while going through the breath):
   _____

2. **Performance Statement** (short, powerful statement that will keep you in the present and remind you of what you have to do to succeed):
   _____
   _____
   _____
   _____

3. **Self Image Booster** (a future statement outlining something you are going to do):
   _____
   _____
   _____
   _____
   _____

4. **Active Visualization Video** (this is your internal video you will run in your head before training sessions):
   a. **First 60 seconds:**
      _____
      _____
      _____

   b. **Second 60 seconds:**
      _____
      _____
      _____

   c. **Third 60 seconds:**
      _____
      _____
      _____

5. **Index cards and implementation:** Now take your mental routine and copy it onto at least two index cards, for your shooting bag, and dry fire area. Now you will have three copies, including this logbook. Ensure you review, and utilize your mental routine each time.

Dry Fire Performance Logs

"Drills build skills….and dry fire is the key"

Competition Handgun Training Logbook

Instructions: These training session log sheets are general in design and will allow you to record your training sessions, and all critical and relevant information. Each section has a specific purpose, and here are some guidelines for each section:

- **Training session name.** This is normally reserved for labeling the session you did. In my book, "Your Competition Handgun Training Program", I assign several different sessions. If you do own that book and follow them, simply label the session you did by key details, such as: "IDPA general", or "Steel Challenge preparation" etc.

- **Preparing for.** Document what you are preparing for, which will help you make more sense of why you might be doing certain drills.

- **Gun/Gear.** It is important that you can look back and check what your MTTS times are for each set of gear you train with. While I recommend sticking with one thing, those of us who train for multiple sports do not have that luxury. Also, some of you might be dry firing for combative purposes, and you might have two carry methods (again not recommended, but realistic for extreme climates).

- **Dry Fire Drill.** Document the specific drill you are doing here. I design and use the exact same drills each time, so that I can track my progress and improvement.

- **Beginning MTTS PAR Time.** This is the PAR time you started the drill with (usually the last time you accomplished in the last session, or a bit slower).

- **Ending MTTS PAR Time.** This is the time you worked your way down to. Initially this time should always be lower (faster), but as you reach higher levels you will see less improvement.

- **Today's Goal Statement.** I like to write a short paragraph or sentence about where I want to go, (and end goal), in a positive first person type statement. Get creative here, and use it to boost your confidence.

- **Notes.** Anything else you want to remember should be written here. If you performed poorly or great does not really matter in the long run, unless you can begin to understand the factors that cause those performances.

There are 10 lines for drills, so you can do and document 10 different drills in each dry fire session. If you are doing more than that, you are either VERY motivated, or possibly not paying attention to detail and doing deliberate practice. I recommend less time with increased focus and intensity to keep you interested and learning.

Don't forget:

- Go through your *Focus Breath* and *Success Visualization Video*
- Review your *Performance Statement* and use it before repetitions
- Review your *Self Image Booster*
- **Stay mentally connected**

Now go dry fire, log your improvement, and work your way to the goals you have set!!

A reminder of your dry-fire training program (for the full program purchase *Your Competition Handgun Training Program*). The following sheets are pre-formatted and each has the dry-fire routine you should be doing that day on them. There are also some open drill slots in case you decide to do additional drills.

Session	Session A (DRAWING SKILLS) [Monday and Wednesday]	Session B (RELOADING SKILLS) [Tuesday and Thursday]	Session C (SPECIALTY SKILLS) [Friday]
Drill's	*ALL SESSIONS WILL BE DONE WITH **3 SETS** FOR EACH SKILL, ONE DONE AT THE TTS (TECHNICAL TRAINING SPEED), ONE DONE AT MTTS (MAXIMUM TECHNICAL TRAINING SPEED), AND ONE DONE TRYING TO "CATCH THE TIMER" (DROPPING TIME IN INCREMENTS)*		
	Stationary Draw Hands Relaxed	Stationary Reload	Draw and Transfer
	Stationary Draw Wrists Above Shoulders	Stepping Reload	Reload and Transfer
	Stationary Draw Barricade	Swinging Reload	Target Acquisitions
	Pivoting Draw	Table Reload	Pick up and Load
	Stepping Draw	IDPA Reloads (Note: only trained if IDPA competitor)	Draw to Alternate Position
	Table Draw		
Total Time	30 minutes	30 minutes	30 minutes

Session/Phase: *A- (Drawing Skills)*   Date: _____

Before you begin remember:

- ➢ Quality is the key to success.
- ➢ Push yourself to the next level, but pay attention to performing proper repetitions.

Gun/Gear (IDPA, USPSA, Etc.):			
Dry Fire Drill		*Beginning MTTS PAR Time*	*Ending MTTS PAR Time*
Stationary Draw Hands Relaxed			
Stationary Draw Wrists Above Shoulders			
Stationary Draw Barricade			
Pivoting Draw			
Stepping Draw			
Table Draw			

Today's goal statement: (Where I want to go)

_____
_____
_____
_____
_____

Notes: (Gun, gear, your performance)

_____
_____
_____
_____
_____
_____

Competition Handgun Training Logbook

Session/Phase: *B (Reloading Skills)*   Date: _____

Before you begin remember:

- ➤ Quality is the key to success.
- ➤ Push yourself to the next level, but pay attention to performing proper repetitions.

Gun/Gear (IDPA, USPSA, Etc.):			
Dry Fire Drill		*Beginning MTTS PAR Time*	*Ending MTTS PAR Time*
Stationary Reload			
Stepping Reload			
Swinging Reload			
Table Reload			
IDPA Reload (reload with retention) **			
IDPA Reload (slidelock)**			

** IDPA Reloads only for those training in that sport

Today's goal statement: (Where I want to go)

_____

_____

_____

_____

_____

Notes: (Gun, gear, your performance)

_____

_____

_____

_____

_____

_____

Copyright 2013, All rights reserved   www.shooting-performance.com

Session/Phase: *A- (Drawing Skills)*   Date: _____

Before you begin remember:

> - Quality is the key to success.
> - Push yourself to the next level, but pay attention to performing proper repetitions.

Gun/Gear (IDPA, USPSA, Etc.):			
Dry Fire Drill		**Beginning MTTS PAR Time**	**Ending MTTS PAR Time**
Stationary Draw Hands Relaxed			
Stationary Draw Wrists Above Shoulders			
Stationary Draw Barricade			
Pivoting Draw			
Stepping Draw			
Table Draw			

Today's goal statement: (Where I want to go)

_____
_____
_____
_____
_____
_____

Notes: (Gun, gear, your performance)

_____
_____
_____
_____
_____
_____
_____

Competition Handgun Training Logbook

Session/Phase: *B (Reloading Skills)*   Date: _____

Before you begin remember:

- ➢ Quality is the key to success.
- ➢ Push yourself to the next level, but pay attention to performing proper repetitions.

Gun/Gear (IDPA, USPSA, Etc.):			
Dry Fire Drill		*Beginning MTTS PAR Time*	*Ending MTTS PAR Time*
Stationary Reload			
Stepping Reload			
Swinging Reload			
Table Reload			
IDPA Reload (reload with retention) **			
IDPA Reload (slidelock)**			
*** IDPA Reloads only for those training in that sport*			

Today's goal statement: (Where I want to go)

_____
_____
_____
_____
_____
_____

Notes: (Gun, gear, your performance)

_____
_____
_____
_____
_____
_____

Competition Handgun Training Logbook

Session/Phase: *C (Specialty Skills)*   Date: _____

Before you begin remember:

- ➢ Quality is the key to success.
- ➢ Push yourself to the next level, but pay attention to performing proper repetitions.

Gun/Gear (IDPA, USPSA, Etc.):			
Dry Fire Drill		*Beginning MTTS PAR Time*	*Ending MTTS PAR Time*
Draw and Transfer			
Reload and Transfer			
Target Acquisitions			
Pick up and Load			
Draw to Alternate Position			

Today's goal statement: (Where I want to go)

_____
_____
_____
_____
_____

Notes: (Gun, gear, your performance)

_____
_____
_____
_____
_____
_____

Competition Handgun Training Logbook

Session/Phase: *A- (Drawing Skills)*   Date: _____

Before you begin remember:

- ➢ Quality is the key to success.
- ➢ Push yourself to the next level, but pay attention to performing proper repetitions.

Gun/Gear (IDPA, USPSA, Etc.):			
Dry Fire Drill		*Beginning MTTS PAR Time*	*Ending MTTS PAR Time*
Stationary Draw Hands Relaxed			
Stationary Draw Wrists Above Shoulders			
Stationary Draw Barricade			
Pivoting Draw			
Stepping Draw			
Table Draw			

Today's goal statement: (Where I want to go)

_____
_____
_____
_____
_____
_____

Notes: (Gun, gear, your performance)

_____
_____
_____
_____
_____
_____
_____

Competition Handgun Training Logbook

Session/Phase: *B (Reloading Skills)*   Date: _____

Before you begin remember:

- Quality is the key to success.
- Push yourself to the next level, but pay attention to performing proper repetitions.

Gun/Gear (IDPA, USPSA, Etc.):			
Dry Fire Drill		*Beginning MTTS PAR Time*	*Ending MTTS PAR Time*
Stationary Reload			
Stepping Reload			
Swinging Reload			
Table Reload			
IDPA Reload (reload with retention) **			
IDPA Reload (slidelock)**			
** IDPA Reloads only for those training in that sport			

Today's goal statement: (Where I want to go)

_____
_____
_____
_____
_____
_____

Notes: (Gun, gear, your performance)

_____
_____
_____
_____
_____
_____
_____

Competition Handgun Training Logbook

Session/Phase: *A- (Drawing Skills)*   Date: _____

Before you begin remember:

- ➢ Quality is the key to success.
- ➢ Push yourself to the next level, but pay attention to performing proper repetitions.

Gun/Gear (IDPA, USPSA, Etc.):		
Dry Fire Drill	*Beginning MTTS PAR Time*	*Ending MTTS PAR Time*
Stationary Draw Hands Relaxed		
Stationary Draw Wrists Above Shoulders		
Stationary Draw Barricade		
Pivoting Draw		
Stepping Draw		
Table Draw		

Today's goal statement: (Where I want to go)

_____
_____
_____
_____
_____

Notes: (Gun, gear, your performance)

_____
_____
_____
_____
_____
_____

Competition Handgun Training Logbook

Session/Phase: *B (Reloading Skills)*   Date: _____

Before you begin remember:

> Quality is the key to success.
> Push yourself to the next level, but pay attention to performing proper repetitions.

Gun/Gear (IDPA, USPSA, Etc.):			
Dry Fire Drill		*Beginning MTTS PAR Time*	*Ending MTTS PAR Time*
Stationary Reload			
Stepping Reload			
Swinging Reload			
Table Reload			
IDPA Reload (reload with retention) **			
IDPA Reload (slidelock)**			
*** IDPA Reloads only for those training in that sport*			

Today's goal statement: (Where I want to go)

_____
_____
_____
_____
_____

Notes: (Gun, gear, your performance)

_____
_____
_____
_____
_____
_____

Session/Phase: *C (Specialty Skills)*   Date: _____

Before you begin remember:

- ➤ Quality is the key to success.
- ➤ Push yourself to the next level, but pay attention to performing proper repetitions.

Gun/Gear (IDPA, USPSA, Etc.):		
Dry Fire Drill	*Beginning MTTS PAR Time*	*Ending MTTS PAR Time*
Draw and Transfer		
Reload and Transfer		
Target Acquisitions		
Pick up and Load		
Draw to Alternate Position		

Today's goal statement: (Where I want to go)

_____
_____
_____
_____
_____

Notes: (Gun, gear, your performance)

_____
_____
_____
_____
_____
_____

Competition Handgun Training Logbook

Session/Phase: *A- (Drawing Skills)*   Date: _____

Before you begin remember:

> ➢ Quality is the key to success.
> ➢ Push yourself to the next level, but pay attention to performing proper repetitions.

Gun/Gear (IDPA, USPSA, Etc.):			
Dry Fire Drill		**Beginning MTTS PAR Time**	**Ending MTTS PAR Time**
Stationary Draw Hands Relaxed			
Stationary Draw Wrists Above Shoulders			
Stationary Draw Barricade			
Pivoting Draw			
Stepping Draw			
Table Draw			

Today's goal statement: (Where I want to go)

_____
_____
_____
_____
_____

Notes: (Gun, gear, your performance)

_____
_____
_____
_____
_____
_____

Competition Handgun Training Logbook

Session/Phase: *B (Reloading Skills)*   Date: _____

Before you begin remember:

- ➢ Quality is the key to success.
- ➢ Push yourself to the next level, but pay attention to performing proper repetitions.

Gun/Gear (IDPA, USPSA, Etc.):			
Dry Fire Drill		*Beginning MTTS PAR Time*	*Ending MTTS PAR Time*
Stationary Reload			
Stepping Reload			
Swinging Reload			
Table Reload			
IDPA Reload (reload with retention) **			
IDPA Reload (slidelock)**			
** *IDPA Reloads only for those training in that sport*			

Today's goal statement: (Where I want to go)

_____

_____

_____

_____

_____

Notes: (Gun, gear, your performance)

_____

_____

_____

_____

_____

_____

_____

Competition Handgun Training Logbook

Session/Phase: *A- (Drawing Skills)*   Date: _____

Before you begin remember:

- ➤ Quality is the key to success.
- ➤ Push yourself to the next level, but pay attention to performing proper repetitions.

Gun/Gear (IDPA, USPSA, Etc.):			
Dry Fire Drill		*Beginning MTTS PAR Time*	*Ending MTTS PAR Time*
Stationary Draw Hands Relaxed			
Stationary Draw Wrists Above Shoulders			
Stationary Draw Barricade			
Pivoting Draw			
Stepping Draw			
Table Draw			

Today's goal statement: (Where I want to go)

_____
_____
_____
_____
_____
_____

Notes: (Gun, gear, your performance)

_____
_____
_____
_____
_____
_____
_____

Competition Handgun Training Logbook

Session/Phase: *B (Reloading Skills)*   Date: _____

Before you begin remember:

- ➢ Quality is the key to success.
- ➢ Push yourself to the next level, but pay attention to performing proper repetitions.

Gun/Gear (IDPA, USPSA, Etc.):			
Dry Fire Drill		*Beginning MTTS PAR Time*	*Ending MTTS PAR Time*
Stationary Reload			
Stepping Reload			
Swinging Reload			
Table Reload			
IDPA Reload (reload with retention) **			
IDPA Reload (slidelock)**			
*** IDPA Reloads only for those training in that sport**			

Today's goal statement: (Where I want to go)

_____

_____

_____

_____

_____

Notes: (Gun, gear, your performance)

_____

_____

_____

_____

_____

_____

Competition Handgun Training Logbook

Session/Phase: *C (Specialty Skills)*   Date: _____

Before you begin remember:

> ➤ Quality is the key to success.
> ➤ Push yourself to the next level, but pay attention to performing proper repetitions.

Gun/Gear (IDPA, USPSA, Etc.):		
Dry Fire Drill	***Beginning MTTS PAR Time***	***Ending MTTS PAR Time***
Draw and Transfer		
Reload and Transfer		
Target Acquisitions		
Pick up and Load		
Draw to Alternate Position		

Today's goal statement: (Where I want to go)

_____
_____
_____
_____
_____

Notes: (Gun, gear, your performance)

_____
_____
_____
_____
_____
_____
_____

Competition Handgun Training Logbook

Session/Phase: *A- (Drawing Skills)*   Date: _____

Before you begin remember:

- ➢ Quality is the key to success.
- ➢ Push yourself to the next level, but pay attention to performing proper repetitions.

Gun/Gear (IDPA, USPSA, Etc.):		
Dry Fire Drill	*Beginning MTTS PAR Time*	*Ending MTTS PAR Time*
Stationary Draw Hands Relaxed		
Stationary Draw Wrists Above Shoulders		
Stationary Draw Barricade		
Pivoting Draw		
Stepping Draw		
Table Draw		

Today's goal statement: (Where I want to go)

_____
_____
_____
_____
_____

Notes: (Gun, gear, your performance)

_____
_____
_____
_____
_____
_____

Session/Phase: B (Reloading Skills)   Date: _____

Before you begin remember:

- Quality is the key to success.
- Push yourself to the next level, but pay attention to performing proper repetitions.

Gun/Gear (IDPA, USPSA, Etc.):			
Dry Fire Drill		***Beginning MTTS PAR Time***	***Ending MTTS PAR Time***
Stationary Reload			
Stepping Reload			
Swinging Reload			
Table Reload			
IDPA Reload (reload with retention) **			
IDPA Reload (slidelock)**			
***** IDPA Reloads only for those training in that sport**			

Today's goal statement: (Where I want to go)

_____
_____
_____
_____
_____

Notes: (Gun, gear, your performance)

_____
_____
_____
_____
_____
_____

Session/Phase: *A- (Drawing Skills)*   Date: _____

Before you begin remember:

- ➤ Quality is the key to success.
- ➤ Push yourself to the next level, but pay attention to performing proper repetitions.

Gun/Gear (IDPA, USPSA, Etc.):			
Dry Fire Drill		*Beginning MTTS PAR Time*	*Ending MTTS PAR Time*
Stationary Draw Hands Relaxed			
Stationary Draw Wrists Above Shoulders			
Stationary Draw Barricade			
Pivoting Draw			
Stepping Draw			
Table Draw			

Today's goal statement: (Where I want to go)

_____
_____
_____
_____
_____
_____

Notes: (Gun, gear, your performance)

_____
_____
_____
_____
_____
_____

Session/Phase: *B (Reloading Skills)*   Date: _____

Before you begin remember:

- Quality is the key to success.
- Push yourself to the next level, but pay attention to performing proper repetitions.

Gun/Gear (IDPA, USPSA, Etc.):			
Dry Fire Drill		*Beginning MTTS PAR Time*	*Ending MTTS PAR Time*
Stationary Reload			
Stepping Reload			
Swinging Reload			
Table Reload			
IDPA Reload (reload with retention) **			
IDPA Reload (slidelock)**			

** IDPA Reloads only for those training in that sport

Today's goal statement: (Where I want to go)

_____
_____
_____
_____
_____

Notes: (Gun, gear, your performance)

_____
_____
_____
_____
_____
_____

Competition Handgun Training Logbook

Session/Phase: *C (Specialty Skills)*   Date: _____

Before you begin remember:

- ➢ Quality is the key to success.
- ➢ Push yourself to the next level, but pay attention to performing proper repetitions.

Gun/Gear (IDPA, USPSA, Etc.):			
Dry Fire Drill		*Beginning MTTS PAR Time*	*Ending MTTS PAR Time*
Draw and Transfer			
Reload and Transfer			
Target Acquisitions			
Pick up and Load			
Draw to Alternate Position			

Today's goal statement: (Where I want to go)

_____
_____
_____
_____
_____

Notes: (Gun, gear, your performance)

_____
_____
_____
_____
_____
_____

Competition Handgun Training Logbook

Session/Phase: *A- (Drawing Skills)*   Date: _____

Before you begin remember:

- ➢ Quality is the key to success.
- ➢ Push yourself to the next level, but pay attention to performing proper repetitions.

Gun/Gear (IDPA, USPSA, Etc.):			
Dry Fire Drill		*Beginning MTTS PAR Time*	*Ending MTTS PAR Time*
Stationary Draw Hands Relaxed			
Stationary Draw Wrists Above Shoulders			
Stationary Draw Barricade			
Pivoting Draw			
Stepping Draw			
Table Draw			

Today's goal statement: (Where I want to go)

_____
_____
_____
_____
_____
_____

Notes: (Gun, gear, your performance)

_____
_____
_____
_____
_____
_____
_____
_____

Competition Handgun Training Logbook

Session/Phase: *B (Reloading Skills)*   Date: _____

Before you begin remember:

> - Quality is the key to success.
> - Push yourself to the next level, but pay attention to performing proper repetitions.

Gun/Gear (IDPA, USPSA, Etc.):			
Dry Fire Drill		***Beginning MTTS PAR Time***	***Ending MTTS PAR Time***
Stationary Reload			
Stepping Reload			
Swinging Reload			
Table Reload			
IDPA Reload (reload with retention) **			
IDPA Reload (slidelock)**			
***** IDPA Reloads only for those training in that sport*			

Today's goal statement: (Where I want to go)

_____
_____
_____
_____
_____

Notes: (Gun, gear, your performance)

_____
_____
_____
_____
_____

Competition Handgun Training Logbook

Session/Phase: *A- (Drawing Skills)*   Date: _____

Before you begin remember:

- ➢ Quality is the key to success.
- ➢ Push yourself to the next level, but pay attention to performing proper repetitions.

Gun/Gear (IDPA, USPSA, Etc.):			
Dry Fire Drill		*Beginning MTTS PAR Time*	*Ending MTTS PAR Time*
Stationary Draw Hands Relaxed			
Stationary Draw Wrists Above Shoulders			
Stationary Draw Barricade			
Pivoting Draw			
Stepping Draw			
Table Draw			

Today's goal statement: (Where I want to go)

_____
_____
_____
_____
_____
_____

Notes: (Gun, gear, your performance)

_____
_____
_____
_____
_____
_____
_____

Session/Phase: B *(Reloading Skills)*   Date: _____

Before you begin remember:

- ➢ Quality is the key to success.
- ➢ Push yourself to the next level, but pay attention to performing proper repetitions.

Gun/Gear (IDPA, USPSA, Etc.):			
Dry Fire Drill		*Beginning MTTS PAR Time*	*Ending MTTS PAR Time*
Stationary Reload			
Stepping Reload			
Swinging Reload			
Table Reload			
IDPA Reload (reload with retention) **			
IDPA Reload (slidelock)**			
*** IDPA Reloads only for those training in that sport*			

Today's goal statement: (Where I want to go)

_____
_____
_____
_____
_____

Notes: (Gun, gear, your performance)

_____
_____
_____
_____
_____

Competition Handgun Training Logbook

Session/Phase: *C (Specialty Skills)*   Date: _____

Before you begin remember:

- ➤ Quality is the key to success.
- ➤ Push yourself to the next level, but pay attention to performing proper repetitions.

Gun/Gear (IDPA, USPSA, Etc.):		
Dry Fire Drill	*Beginning MTTS PAR Time*	*Ending MTTS PAR Time*
Draw and Transfer		
Reload and Transfer		
Target Acquisitions		
Pick up and Load		
Draw to Alternate Position		

Today's goal statement: (Where I want to go)

_____
_____
_____
_____
_____

Notes: (Gun, gear, your performance)

_____
_____
_____
_____
_____
_____
_____

Competition Handgun Training Logbook

Session/Phase: A- *(Drawing Skills)*   Date: _____

Before you begin remember:

- ➢ Quality is the key to success.
- ➢ Push yourself to the next level, but pay attention to performing proper repetitions.

Gun/Gear (IDPA, USPSA, Etc.):			
Dry Fire Drill		*Beginning MTTS PAR Time*	*Ending MTTS PAR Time*
Stationary Draw Hands Relaxed			
Stationary Draw Wrists Above Shoulders			
Stationary Draw Barricade			
Pivoting Draw			
Stepping Draw			
Table Draw			

Today's goal statement: (Where I want to go)

_____

_____

_____

_____

_____

Notes: (Gun, gear, your performance)

_____

_____

_____

_____

_____

_____

Session/Phase: *B (Reloading Skills)*   Date: _____

Before you begin remember:

- ➢ Quality is the key to success.
- ➢ Push yourself to the next level, but pay attention to performing proper repetitions.

Gun/Gear (IDPA, USPSA, Etc.):			
Dry Fire Drill		*Beginning MTTS PAR Time*	*Ending MTTS PAR Time*
Stationary Reload			
Stepping Reload			
Swinging Reload			
Table Reload			
IDPA Reload (reload with retention) **			
IDPA Reload (slidelock)**			
*** IDPA Reloads only for those training in that sport*			

Today's goal statement: (Where I want to go)

_____
_____
_____
_____
_____

Notes: (Gun, gear, your performance)

_____
_____
_____
_____
_____
_____

Competition Handgun Training Logbook

Session/Phase: A- *(Drawing Skills)*   Date: _____

Before you begin remember:

- ➢ Quality is the key to success.
- ➢ Push yourself to the next level, but pay attention to performing proper repetitions.

Gun/Gear (IDPA, USPSA, Etc.):		
Dry Fire Drill	*Beginning MTTS PAR Time*	*Ending MTTS PAR Time*
Stationary Draw Hands Relaxed		
Stationary Draw Wrists Above Shoulders		
Stationary Draw Barricade		
Pivoting Draw		
Stepping Draw		
Table Draw		

Today's goal statement: (Where I want to go)

_____
_____
_____
_____
_____

Notes: (Gun, gear, your performance)

_____
_____
_____
_____
_____
_____

Competition Handgun Training Logbook

Session/Phase: *B (Reloading Skills)*   Date: _____

Before you begin remember:

- Quality is the key to success.
- Push yourself to the next level, but pay attention to performing proper repetitions.

Gun/Gear (IDPA, USPSA, Etc.):			
Dry Fire Drill		*Beginning MTTS PAR Time*	*Ending MTTS PAR Time*
Stationary Reload			
Stepping Reload			
Swinging Reload			
Table Reload			
IDPA Reload (reload with retention) **			
IDPA Reload (slidelock)**			
** *IDPA Reloads only for those training in that sport*			

Today's goal statement: (Where I want to go)

_____
_____
_____
_____
_____

Notes: (Gun, gear, your performance)

_____
_____
_____
_____
_____
_____

Session/Phase: *C (Specialty Skills)*   Date: _____

Before you begin remember:

- ➢ Quality is the key to success.
- ➢ Push yourself to the next level, but pay attention to performing proper repetitions.

Gun/Gear (IDPA, USPSA, Etc.):		
Dry Fire Drill	*Beginning MTTS PAR Time*	*Ending MTTS PAR Time*
Draw and Transfer		
Reload and Transfer		
Target Acquisitions		
Pick up and Load		
Draw to Alternate Position		

Today's goal statement: (Where I want to go)

_____
_____
_____
_____
_____

Notes: (Gun, gear, your performance)

_____
_____
_____
_____
_____
_____

Competition Handgun Training Logbook

Session/Phase: *A- (Drawing Skills)*   Date: _____

Before you begin remember:

- ➢ Quality is the key to success.
- ➢ Push yourself to the next level, but pay attention to performing proper repetitions.

Gun/Gear (IDPA, USPSA, Etc.):			
Dry Fire Drill		*Beginning MTTS PAR Time*	*Ending MTTS PAR Time*
Stationary Draw Hands Relaxed			
Stationary Draw Wrists Above Shoulders			
Stationary Draw Barricade			
Pivoting Draw			
Stepping Draw			
Table Draw			

Today's goal statement: (Where I want to go)

_____
_____
_____
_____
_____
_____

Notes: (Gun, gear, your performance)

_____
_____
_____
_____
_____
_____

Session/Phase: *B (Reloading Skills)*   Date: _____

Before you begin remember:

- ➢ Quality is the key to success.
- ➢ Push yourself to the next level, but pay attention to performing proper repetitions.

Gun/Gear (IDPA, USPSA, Etc.):			
Dry Fire Drill		*Beginning MTTS PAR Time*	*Ending MTTS PAR Time*
Stationary Reload			
Stepping Reload			
Swinging Reload			
Table Reload			
IDPA Reload (reload with retention) **			
IDPA Reload (slidelock)**			
*** IDPA Reloads only for those training in that sport***			

Today's goal statement: (Where I want to go)

_____
_____
_____
_____
_____
_____

Notes: (Gun, gear, your performance)

_____
_____
_____
_____
_____
_____
_____

Session/Phase: A- *(Drawing Skills)*   Date: _____

Before you begin remember:

- ➢ Quality is the key to success.
- ➢ Push yourself to the next level, but pay attention to performing proper repetitions.

Gun/Gear (IDPA, USPSA, Etc.):		
Dry Fire Drill	***Beginning MTTS PAR Time***	***Ending MTTS PAR Time***
Stationary Draw Hands Relaxed		
Stationary Draw Wrists Above Shoulders		
Stationary Draw Barricade		
Pivoting Draw		
Stepping Draw		
Table Draw		

Today's goal statement: (Where I want to go)

_____
_____
_____
_____
_____

Notes: (Gun, gear, your performance)

_____
_____
_____
_____
_____
_____

Competition Handgun Training Logbook

Session/Phase: *B (Reloading Skills)*   Date: _____

Before you begin remember:

- ➢ Quality is the key to success.
- ➢ Push yourself to the next level, but pay attention to performing proper repetitions.

Gun/Gear (IDPA, USPSA, Etc.):			
Dry Fire Drill		*Beginning MTTS PAR Time*	*Ending MTTS PAR Time*
Stationary Reload			
Stepping Reload			
Swinging Reload			
Table Reload			
IDPA Reload (reload with retention) **			
IDPA Reload (slidelock)**			
*** IDPA Reloads only for those training in that sport*			

Today's goal statement: (Where I want to go)

_____
_____
_____
_____
_____

Notes: (Gun, gear, your performance)

_____
_____
_____
_____
_____
_____

Competition Handgun Training Logbook

Session/Phase: *C (Specialty Skills)*   Date: _____

Before you begin remember:

- ➢ Quality is the key to success.
- ➢ Push yourself to the next level, but pay attention to performing proper repetitions.

Gun/Gear (IDPA, USPSA, Etc.):			
Dry Fire Drill		*Beginning MTTS PAR Time*	*Ending MTTS PAR Time*
Draw and Transfer			
Reload and Transfer			
Target Acquisitions			
Pick up and Load			
Draw to Alternate Position			

Today's goal statement: (Where I want to go)

_____
_____
_____
_____
_____
_____

Notes: (Gun, gear, your performance)

_____
_____
_____
_____
_____
_____
_____

Competition Handgun Training Logbook

Session/Phase: *A- (Drawing Skills)*   Date: _____

Before you begin remember:

- ➢ Quality is the key to success.
- ➢ Push yourself to the next level, but pay attention to performing proper repetitions.

Gun/Gear (IDPA, USPSA, Etc.):			
Dry Fire Drill		*Beginning MTTS PAR Time*	*Ending MTTS PAR Time*
Stationary Draw Hands Relaxed			
Stationary Draw Wrists Above Shoulders			
Stationary Draw Barricade			
Pivoting Draw			
Stepping Draw			
Table Draw			

Today's goal statement: (Where I want to go)

_____
_____
_____
_____
_____
_____

Notes: (Gun, gear, your performance)

_____
_____
_____
_____
_____
_____

Competition Handgun Training Logbook

Session/Phase: *B (Reloading Skills)*   Date: _____

Before you begin remember:

- ➢ Quality is the key to success.
- ➢ Push yourself to the next level, but pay attention to performing proper repetitions.

Gun/Gear (IDPA, USPSA, Etc.):			
Dry Fire Drill		*Beginning MTTS PAR Time*	*Ending MTTS PAR Time*
Stationary Reload			
Stepping Reload			
Swinging Reload			
Table Reload			
IDPA Reload (reload with retention) **			
IDPA Reload (slidelock)**			
*** IDPA Reloads only for those training in that sport*			

Today's goal statement: (Where I want to go)

_____
_____
_____
_____
_____

Notes: (Gun, gear, your performance)

_____
_____
_____
_____
_____
_____
_____

Competition Handgun Training Logbook

Session/Phase: A- *(Drawing Skills)*   Date: _____

Before you begin remember:

- ➢ Quality is the key to success.
- ➢ Push yourself to the next level, but pay attention to performing proper repetitions.

Gun/Gear (IDPA, USPSA, Etc.):			
Dry Fire Drill		*Beginning MTTS PAR Time*	*Ending MTTS PAR Time*
Stationary Draw Hands Relaxed			
Stationary Draw Wrists Above Shoulders			
Stationary Draw Barricade			
Pivoting Draw			
Stepping Draw			
Table Draw			

Today's goal statement: (Where I want to go)

_____
_____
_____
_____
_____

Notes: (Gun, gear, your performance)

_____
_____
_____
_____
_____
_____

Competition Handgun Training Logbook

Session/Phase: *B (Reloading Skills)*   Date: _____

Before you begin remember:

- ➢ Quality is the key to success.
- ➢ Push yourself to the next level, but pay attention to performing proper repetitions.

Gun/Gear (IDPA, USPSA, Etc.):			
Dry Fire Drill		*Beginning MTTS PAR Time*	*Ending MTTS PAR Time*
Stationary Reload			
Stepping Reload			
Swinging Reload			
Table Reload			
IDPA Reload (reload with retention) **			
IDPA Reload (slidelock)**			

*** IDPA Reloads only for those training in that sport**

Today's goal statement: (Where I want to go)

_____
_____
_____
_____
_____

Notes: (Gun, gear, your performance)

_____
_____
_____
_____
_____
_____

Competition Handgun Training Logbook

Session/Phase: *C (Specialty Skills)*   Date: _____

Before you begin remember:

- ➢ Quality is the key to success.
- ➢ Push yourself to the next level, but pay attention to performing proper repetitions.

Gun/Gear (IDPA, USPSA, Etc.):			
Dry Fire Drill		*Beginning MTTS PAR Time*	*Ending MTTS PAR Time*
Draw and Transfer			
Reload and Transfer			
Target Acquisitions			
Pick up and Load			
Draw to Alternate Position			

Today's goal statement: (Where I want to go)

_____
_____
_____
_____
_____

Notes: (Gun, gear, your performance)

_____
_____
_____
_____
_____

Session/Phase: *A- (Drawing Skills)*   Date: _____

Before you begin remember:

> ➤ Quality is the key to success.
> ➤ Push yourself to the next level, but pay attention to performing proper repetitions.

Gun/Gear (IDPA, USPSA, Etc.):		
Dry Fire Drill	*Beginning MTTS PAR Time*	*Ending MTTS PAR Time*
Stationary Draw Hands Relaxed		
Stationary Draw Wrists Above Shoulders		
Stationary Draw Barricade		
Pivoting Draw		
Stepping Draw		
Table Draw		

Today's goal statement: (Where I want to go)

_____
_____
_____
_____
_____

Notes: (Gun, gear, your performance)

_____
_____
_____
_____
_____
_____

Session/Phase: B (Reloading Skills)   Date: _____

Before you begin remember:

- Quality is the key to success.
- Push yourself to the next level, but pay attention to performing proper repetitions.

Gun/Gear (IDPA, USPSA, Etc.):			
Dry Fire Drill		*Beginning MTTS PAR Time*	*Ending MTTS PAR Time*
Stationary Reload			
Stepping Reload			
Swinging Reload			
Table Reload			
IDPA Reload (reload with retention) **			
IDPA Reload (slidelock)**			
** *IDPA Reloads only for those training in that sport*			

Today's goal statement: (Where I want to go)

_____
_____
_____
_____
_____
_____

Notes: (Gun, gear, your performance)

_____
_____
_____
_____
_____
_____
_____

Competition Handgun Training Logbook

Session/Phase: *A- (Drawing Skills)*   Date: _____

Before you begin remember:

- ➢ Quality is the key to success.
- ➢ Push yourself to the next level, but pay attention to performing proper repetitions.

Gun/Gear (IDPA, USPSA, Etc.):		
Dry Fire Drill	*Beginning MTTS PAR Time*	*Ending MTTS PAR Time*
Stationary Draw Hands Relaxed		
Stationary Draw Wrists Above Shoulders		
Stationary Draw Barricade		
Pivoting Draw		
Stepping Draw		
Table Draw		

Today's goal statement: (Where I want to go)

_____
_____
_____
_____
_____

Notes: (Gun, gear, your performance)

_____
_____
_____
_____
_____
_____
_____

Session/Phase: B (Reloading Skills)   Date: _____

Before you begin remember:

- ➢ Quality is the key to success.
- ➢ Push yourself to the next level, but pay attention to performing proper repetitions.

Gun/Gear (IDPA, USPSA, Etc.):			
Dry Fire Drill		*Beginning MTTS PAR Time*	*Ending MTTS PAR Time*
Stationary Reload			
Stepping Reload			
Swinging Reload			
Table Reload			
IDPA Reload (reload with retention) **			
IDPA Reload (slidelock)**			
*** IDPA Reloads only for those training in that sport*			

Today's goal statement: (Where I want to go)

_____
_____
_____
_____
_____
_____

Notes: (Gun, gear, your performance)

_____
_____
_____
_____
_____
_____
_____

Competition Handgun Training Logbook

Session/Phase: *C (Specialty Skills)*   Date: _____

Before you begin remember:

- ➢ Quality is the key to success.
- ➢ Push yourself to the next level, but pay attention to performing proper repetitions.

Gun/Gear (IDPA, USPSA, Etc.):			
Dry Fire Drill		*Beginning MTTS PAR Time*	*Ending MTTS PAR Time*
Draw and Transfer			
Reload and Transfer			
Target Acquisitions			
Pick up and Load			
Draw to Alternate Position			

Today's goal statement: (Where I want to go)

_____
_____
_____
_____
_____
_____

Notes: (Gun, gear, your performance)

_____
_____
_____
_____
_____
_____
_____

Session/Phase: A- *(Drawing Skills)*   Date: _____

Before you begin remember:

- ➢ Quality is the key to success.
- ➢ Push yourself to the next level, but pay attention to performing proper repetitions.

Gun/Gear (IDPA, USPSA, Etc.):			
Dry Fire Drill		*Beginning MTTS PAR Time*	*Ending MTTS PAR Time*
Stationary Draw Hands Relaxed			
Stationary Draw Wrists Above Shoulders			
Stationary Draw Barricade			
Pivoting Draw			
Stepping Draw			
Table Draw			

Today's goal statement: (Where I want to go)

_____

_____

_____

_____

_____

Notes: (Gun, gear, your performance)

_____

_____

_____

_____

_____

_____

Competition Handgun Training Logbook

Session/Phase: *B (Reloading Skills)*   Date: _____

Before you begin remember:

- ➢ Quality is the key to success.
- ➢ Push yourself to the next level, but pay attention to performing proper repetitions.

Gun/Gear (IDPA, USPSA, Etc.):			
Dry Fire Drill		*Beginning MTTS PAR Time*	*Ending MTTS PAR Time*
Stationary Reload			
Stepping Reload			
Swinging Reload			
Table Reload			
IDPA Reload (reload with retention) **			
IDPA Reload (slidelock)**			

** *IDPA Reloads only for those training in that sport*

Today's goal statement: (Where I want to go)

_____
_____
_____
_____
_____

Notes: (Gun, gear, your performance)

_____
_____
_____
_____
_____

Session/Phase: *A- (Drawing Skills)*   Date: _____

Before you begin remember:

- ➢ Quality is the key to success.
- ➢ Push yourself to the next level, but pay attention to performing proper repetitions.

Gun/Gear (IDPA, USPSA, Etc.):		
Dry Fire Drill	*Beginning MTTS PAR Time*	*Ending MTTS PAR Time*
Stationary Draw Hands Relaxed		
Stationary Draw Wrists Above Shoulders		
Stationary Draw Barricade		
Pivoting Draw		
Stepping Draw		
Table Draw		

Today's goal statement: (Where I want to go)

_____
_____
_____
_____
_____

Notes: (Gun, gear, your performance)

_____
_____
_____
_____
_____

Competition Handgun Training Logbook

Session/Phase: *B (Reloading Skills)*   Date: _____

Before you begin remember:

> ➢ Quality is the key to success.
> ➢ Push yourself to the next level, but pay attention to performing proper repetitions.

Gun/Gear (IDPA, USPSA, Etc.):			
Dry Fire Drill		*Beginning MTTS PAR Time*	*Ending MTTS PAR Time*
Stationary Reload			
Stepping Reload			
Swinging Reload			
Table Reload			
IDPA Reload (reload with retention) **			
IDPA Reload (slidelock)**			
** *IDPA Reloads only for those training in that sport*			

Today's goal statement: (Where I want to go)

_____
_____
_____
_____
_____

Notes: (Gun, gear, your performance)

_____
_____
_____
_____
_____

Session/Phase: *C (Specialty Skills)*   Date: _____

Before you begin remember:

- ➢ Quality is the key to success.
- ➢ Push yourself to the next level, but pay attention to performing proper repetitions.

Gun/Gear (IDPA, USPSA, Etc.):			
Dry Fire Drill		*Beginning MTTS PAR Time*	*Ending MTTS PAR Time*
Draw and Transfer			
Reload and Transfer			
Target Acquisitions			
Pick up and Load			
Draw to Alternate Position			

Today's goal statement: (Where I want to go)

_____
_____
_____
_____
_____

Notes: (Gun, gear, your performance)

_____
_____
_____
_____
_____
_____

Session/Phase: *A- (Drawing Skills)*   Date: _____

Before you begin remember:

- ➢ Quality is the key to success.
- ➢ Push yourself to the next level, but pay attention to performing proper repetitions.

Gun/Gear (IDPA, USPSA, Etc.):			
Dry Fire Drill		*Beginning MTTS PAR Time*	*Ending MTTS PAR Time*
Stationary Draw Hands Relaxed			
Stationary Draw Wrists Above Shoulders			
Stationary Draw Barricade			
Pivoting Draw			
Stepping Draw			
Table Draw			

Today's goal statement: (Where I want to go)

_____
_____
_____
_____
_____

Notes: (Gun, gear, your performance)

_____
_____
_____
_____
_____
_____
_____

Competition Handgun Training Logbook

Session/Phase: *B (Reloading Skills)*   Date: _____

Before you begin remember:

- ➢ Quality is the key to success.
- ➢ Push yourself to the next level, but pay attention to performing proper repetitions.

Gun/Gear (IDPA, USPSA, Etc.):			
Dry Fire Drill		*Beginning MTTS PAR Time*	*Ending MTTS PAR Time*
Stationary Reload			
Stepping Reload			
Swinging Reload			
Table Reload			
IDPA Reload (reload with retention) **			
IDPA Reload (slidelock)**			
*** IDPA Reloads only for those training in that sport*			

Today's goal statement: (Where I want to go)

_____
_____
_____
_____
_____

Notes: (Gun, gear, your performance)

_____
_____
_____
_____
_____
_____

Competition Handgun Training Logbook

Session/Phase: *A- (Drawing Skills)*   Date: _____

Before you begin remember:

> ➢ Quality is the key to success.
> ➢ Push yourself to the next level, but pay attention to performing proper repetitions.

Gun/Gear (IDPA, USPSA, Etc.):		
Dry Fire Drill	*Beginning MTTS PAR Time*	*Ending MTTS PAR Time*
Stationary Draw Hands Relaxed		
Stationary Draw Wrists Above Shoulders		
Stationary Draw Barricade		
Pivoting Draw		
Stepping Draw		
Table Draw		

Today's goal statement: (Where I want to go)

_____
_____
_____
_____
_____

Notes: (Gun, gear, your performance)

_____
_____
_____
_____
_____
_____

Competition Handgun Training Logbook

Session/Phase: *B (Reloading Skills)*   Date: _____

Before you begin remember:

- ➢ Quality is the key to success.
- ➢ Push yourself to the next level, but pay attention to performing proper repetitions.

Gun/Gear (IDPA, USPSA, Etc.):			
Dry Fire Drill		*Beginning MTTS PAR Time*	*Ending MTTS PAR Time*
Stationary Reload			
Stepping Reload			
Swinging Reload			
Table Reload			
IDPA Reload (reload with retention) **			
IDPA Reload (slidelock)**			
** IDPA Reloads only for those training in that sport			

Today's goal statement: (Where I want to go)

_____
_____
_____
_____
_____

Notes: (Gun, gear, your performance)

_____
_____
_____
_____
_____
_____

Competition Handgun Training Logbook

Session/Phase: *C (Specialty Skills)*   Date: _____

Before you begin remember:

- ➢ Quality is the key to success.
- ➢ Push yourself to the next level, but pay attention to performing proper repetitions.

Gun/Gear (IDPA, USPSA, Etc.):			
Dry Fire Drill		*Beginning MTTS PAR Time*	*Ending MTTS PAR Time*
Draw and Transfer			
Reload and Transfer			
Target Acquisitions			
Pick up and Load			
Draw to Alternate Position			

Today's goal statement: (Where I want to go)

_____
_____
_____
_____
_____

Notes: (Gun, gear, your performance)

_____
_____
_____
_____
_____
_____

Competition Handgun Training Logbook

Session/Phase: *A- (Drawing Skills)*   Date: _____

Before you begin remember:

- ➢ Quality is the key to success.
- ➢ Push yourself to the next level, but pay attention to performing proper repetitions.

Gun/Gear (IDPA, USPSA, Etc.):			
Dry Fire Drill		*Beginning MTTS PAR Time*	*Ending MTTS PAR Time*
Stationary Draw Hands Relaxed			
Stationary Draw Wrists Above Shoulders			
Stationary Draw Barricade			
Pivoting Draw			
Stepping Draw			
Table Draw			

Today's goal statement: (Where I want to go)

_____
_____
_____
_____
_____
_____

Notes: (Gun, gear, your performance)

_____
_____
_____
_____
_____
_____
_____

Competition Handgun Training Logbook

Session/Phase: *B (Reloading Skills)*   Date: _____

Before you begin remember:

➢ Quality is the key to success.
➢ Push yourself to the next level, but pay attention to performing proper repetitions.

Gun/Gear (IDPA, USPSA, Etc.):			
Dry Fire Drill		*Beginning MTTS PAR Time*	*Ending MTTS PAR Time*
Stationary Reload			
Stepping Reload			
Swinging Reload			
Table Reload			
IDPA Reload (reload with retention) **			
IDPA Reload (slidelock)**			
*** IDPA Reloads only for those training in that sport*			

Today's goal statement: (Where I want to go)

_____
_____
_____
_____
_____

Notes: (Gun, gear, your performance)

_____
_____
_____
_____
_____
_____
_____

Session/Phase: *A- (Drawing Skills)*   Date: _____

Before you begin remember:

- ➢ Quality is the key to success.
- ➢ Push yourself to the next level, but pay attention to performing proper repetitions.

Gun/Gear (IDPA, USPSA, Etc.):		
Dry Fire Drill	*Beginning MTTS PAR Time*	*Ending MTTS PAR Time*
Stationary Draw Hands Relaxed		
Stationary Draw Wrists Above Shoulders		
Stationary Draw Barricade		
Pivoting Draw		
Stepping Draw		
Table Draw		

Today's goal statement: (Where I want to go)

_____

_____

_____

_____

_____

Notes: (Gun, gear, your performance)

_____

_____

_____

_____

_____

_____

Competition Handgun Training Logbook

Session/Phase: *B (Reloading Skills)*   Date: _____

Before you begin remember:

- Quality is the key to success.
- Push yourself to the next level, but pay attention to performing proper repetitions.

Gun/Gear (IDPA, USPSA, Etc.):			
Dry Fire Drill		*Beginning MTTS PAR Time*	*Ending MTTS PAR Time*
Stationary Reload			
Stepping Reload			
Swinging Reload			
Table Reload			
IDPA Reload (reload with retention) **			
IDPA Reload (slidelock)**			
*** IDPA Reloads only for those training in that sport*			

Today's goal statement: (Where I want to go)

_____

_____

_____

_____

_____

Notes: (Gun, gear, your performance)

_____

_____

_____

_____

_____

_____

Competition Handgun Training Logbook

Session/Phase: *C (Specialty Skills)*   Date: _____

Before you begin remember:

- ➢ Quality is the key to success.
- ➢ Push yourself to the next level, but pay attention to performing proper repetitions.

Gun/Gear (IDPA, USPSA, Etc.):			
Dry Fire Drill		*Beginning MTTS PAR Time*	*Ending MTTS PAR Time*
Draw and Transfer			
Reload and Transfer			
Target Acquisitions			
Pick up and Load			
Draw to Alternate Position			

Today's goal statement: (Where I want to go)

_____

_____

_____

_____

_____

Notes: (Gun, gear, your performance)

_____

_____

_____

_____

_____

_____

Competition Handgun Training Logbook

Session/Phase: *A- (Drawing Skills)*   Date: _____

Before you begin remember:

- ➢ Quality is the key to success.
- ➢ Push yourself to the next level, but pay attention to performing proper repetitions.

Gun/Gear (IDPA, USPSA, Etc.):			
Dry Fire Drill		*Beginning MTTS PAR Time*	*Ending MTTS PAR Time*
Stationary Draw Hands Relaxed			
Stationary Draw Wrists Above Shoulders			
Stationary Draw Barricade			
Pivoting Draw			
Stepping Draw			
Table Draw			

Today's goal statement: (Where I want to go)

_____
_____
_____
_____
_____

Notes: (Gun, gear, your performance)

_____
_____
_____
_____
_____
_____
_____

Competition Handgun Training Logbook

Session/Phase: *B (Reloading Skills)*   Date: _____

Before you begin remember:

- ➢ Quality is the key to success.
- ➢ Push yourself to the next level, but pay attention to performing proper repetitions.

Gun/Gear (IDPA, USPSA, Etc.):			
Dry Fire Drill		*Beginning MTTS PAR Time*	*Ending MTTS PAR Time*
Stationary Reload			
Stepping Reload			
Swinging Reload			
Table Reload			
IDPA Reload (reload with retention) **			
IDPA Reload (slidelock)**			
*** IDPA Reloads only for those training in that sport*			

Today's goal statement: (Where I want to go)

_____
_____
_____
_____
_____
_____

Notes: (Gun, gear, your performance)

_____
_____
_____
_____
_____
_____
_____

Competition Handgun Training Logbook

Session/Phase: *A- (Drawing Skills)*   Date: _____

Before you begin remember:

- ➤ Quality is the key to success.
- ➤ Push yourself to the next level, but pay attention to performing proper repetitions.

Gun/Gear (IDPA, USPSA, Etc.):			
Dry Fire Drill		*Beginning MTTS PAR Time*	*Ending MTTS PAR Time*
Stationary Draw Hands Relaxed			
Stationary Draw Wrists Above Shoulders			
Stationary Draw Barricade			
Pivoting Draw			
Stepping Draw			
Table Draw			

Today's goal statement: (Where I want to go)

_____
_____
_____
_____
_____

Notes: (Gun, gear, your performance)

_____
_____
_____
_____
_____

Session/Phase: B (Reloading Skills)   Date: _____

Before you begin remember:

- ➢ Quality is the key to success.
- ➢ Push yourself to the next level, but pay attention to performing proper repetitions.

Gun/Gear (IDPA, USPSA, Etc.):		
Dry Fire Drill	***Beginning MTTS PAR Time***	***Ending MTTS PAR Time***
Stationary Reload		
Stepping Reload		
Swinging Reload		
Table Reload		
IDPA Reload (reload with retention) **		
IDPA Reload (slidelock)**		
***** *IDPA Reloads only for those training in that sport*		

Today's goal statement: (Where I want to go)

_____
_____
_____
_____
_____
_____

Notes: (Gun, gear, your performance)

_____
_____
_____
_____
_____
_____
_____

Competition Handgun Training Logbook

Session/Phase: *C (Specialty Skills)*   Date: _____

Before you begin remember:

- ➢ Quality is the key to success.
- ➢ Push yourself to the next level, but pay attention to performing proper repetitions.

Gun/Gear (IDPA, USPSA, Etc.):			
Dry Fire Drill		*Beginning MTTS PAR Time*	*Ending MTTS PAR Time*
Draw and Transfer			
Reload and Transfer			
Target Acquisitions			
Pick up and Load			
Draw to Alternate Position			

Today's goal statement: (Where I want to go)

_____
_____
_____
_____
_____

Notes: (Gun, gear, your performance)

_____
_____
_____
_____
_____
_____

Competition Handgun Training Logbook

Session/Phase: *A- (Drawing Skills)*   Date: _____

Before you begin remember:

- ➤ Quality is the key to success.
- ➤ Push yourself to the next level, but pay attention to performing proper repetitions.

Gun/Gear (IDPA, USPSA, Etc.):			
Dry Fire Drill		*Beginning MTTS PAR Time*	*Ending MTTS PAR Time*
Stationary Draw Hands Relaxed			
Stationary Draw Wrists Above Shoulders			
Stationary Draw Barricade			
Pivoting Draw			
Stepping Draw			
Table Draw			

Today's goal statement: (Where I want to go)

_____

_____

_____

_____

_____

Notes: (Gun, gear, your performance)

_____

_____

_____

_____

_____

_____

Competition Handgun Training Logbook

Session/Phase: *B (Reloading Skills)*   Date: _____

Before you begin remember:

- Quality is the key to success.
- Push yourself to the next level, but pay attention to performing proper repetitions.

Gun/Gear (IDPA, USPSA, Etc.):			
Dry Fire Drill		*Beginning MTTS PAR Time*	*Ending MTTS PAR Time*
Stationary Reload			
Stepping Reload			
Swinging Reload			
Table Reload			
IDPA Reload (reload with retention) **			
IDPA Reload (slidelock)**			

*** IDPA Reloads only for those training in that sport*

Today's goal statement: (Where I want to go)

_____
_____
_____
_____
_____

Notes: (Gun, gear, your performance)

_____
_____
_____
_____
_____
_____

Competition Handgun Training Logbook

Session/Phase: *A- (Drawing Skills)*   Date: _____

Before you begin remember:

- ➢ Quality is the key to success.
- ➢ Push yourself to the next level, but pay attention to performing proper repetitions.

Gun/Gear (IDPA, USPSA, Etc.):			
Dry Fire Drill		*Beginning MTTS PAR Time*	*Ending MTTS PAR Time*
Stationary Draw Hands Relaxed			
Stationary Draw Wrists Above Shoulders			
Stationary Draw Barricade			
Pivoting Draw			
Stepping Draw			
Table Draw			

Today's goal statement: (Where I want to go)

_____
_____
_____
_____
_____
_____

Notes: (Gun, gear, your performance)

_____
_____
_____
_____
_____
_____
_____

Competition Handgun Training Logbook

Session/Phase: *B (Reloading Skills)*   Date: _____

Before you begin remember:

- ➢ Quality is the key to success.
- ➢ Push yourself to the next level, but pay attention to performing proper repetitions.

Gun/Gear (IDPA, USPSA, Etc.):			
Dry Fire Drill		*Beginning MTTS PAR Time*	*Ending MTTS PAR Time*
Stationary Reload			
Stepping Reload			
Swinging Reload			
Table Reload			
IDPA Reload (reload with retention) **			
IDPA Reload (slidelock)**			
** IDPA Reloads only for those training in that sport			

Today's goal statement: (Where I want to go)

_____
_____
_____
_____
_____

Notes: (Gun, gear, your performance)

_____
_____
_____
_____
_____
_____

Competition Handgun Training Logbook

Session/Phase: *C (Specialty Skills)*   Date: _____

Before you begin remember:

- ➢ Quality is the key to success.
- ➢ Push yourself to the next level, but pay attention to performing proper repetitions.

Gun/Gear (IDPA, USPSA, Etc.):			
Dry Fire Drill		*Beginning MTTS PAR Time*	*Ending MTTS PAR Time*
Draw and Transfer			
Reload and Transfer			
Target Acquisitions			
Pick up and Load			
Draw to Alternate Position			

Today's goal statement: (Where I want to go)

_____

_____

_____

_____

_____

Notes: (Gun, gear, your performance)

_____

_____

_____

_____

_____

_____

Competition Handgun Training Logbook

Session/Phase: *A- (Drawing Skills)*   Date: _____

Before you begin remember:

- ➢ Quality is the key to success.
- ➢ Push yourself to the next level, but pay attention to performing proper repetitions.

Gun/Gear (IDPA, USPSA, Etc.):			
Dry Fire Drill		*Beginning MTTS PAR Time*	*Ending MTTS PAR Time*
Stationary Draw Hands Relaxed			
Stationary Draw Wrists Above Shoulders			
Stationary Draw Barricade			
Pivoting Draw			
Stepping Draw			
Table Draw			

Today's goal statement: (Where I want to go)

_____
_____
_____
_____
_____
_____

Notes: (Gun, gear, your performance)

_____
_____
_____
_____
_____
_____
_____

Competition Handgun Training Logbook

Session/Phase: *B (Reloading Skills)*   Date: _____

Before you begin remember:

- ➢ Quality is the key to success.
- ➢ Push yourself to the next level, but pay attention to performing proper repetitions.

Gun/Gear (IDPA, USPSA, Etc.):			
Dry Fire Drill		*Beginning MTTS PAR Time*	*Ending MTTS PAR Time*
Stationary Reload			
Stepping Reload			
Swinging Reload			
Table Reload			
IDPA Reload (reload with retention) **			
IDPA Reload (slidelock)**			
*** IDPA Reloads only for those training in that sport*			

Today's goal statement: (Where I want to go)

_____
_____
_____
_____
_____

Notes: (Gun, gear, your performance)

_____
_____
_____
_____
_____
_____
_____

Competition Handgun Training Logbook

Session/Phase: *A- (Drawing Skills)*   Date: _____

Before you begin remember:

- ➢ Quality is the key to success.
- ➢ Push yourself to the next level, but pay attention to performing proper repetitions.

Gun/Gear (IDPA, USPSA, Etc.):			
Dry Fire Drill		*Beginning MTTS PAR Time*	*Ending MTTS PAR Time*
Stationary Draw Hands Relaxed			
Stationary Draw Wrists Above Shoulders			
Stationary Draw Barricade			
Pivoting Draw			
Stepping Draw			
Table Draw			

Today's goal statement: (Where I want to go)

_____
_____
_____
_____
_____

Notes: (Gun, gear, your performance)

_____
_____
_____
_____
_____
_____

Competition Handgun Training Logbook

Session/Phase: *B (Reloading Skills)*   Date: _____

Before you begin remember:

- ➢ Quality is the key to success.
- ➢ Push yourself to the next level, but pay attention to performing proper repetitions.

Gun/Gear (IDPA, USPSA, Etc.):			
Dry Fire Drill		*Beginning MTTS PAR Time*	*Ending MTTS PAR Time*
Stationary Reload			
Stepping Reload			
Swinging Reload			
Table Reload			
IDPA Reload (reload with retention) **			
IDPA Reload (slidelock)**			
*** IDPA Reloads only for those training in that sport*			

Today's goal statement: (Where I want to go)

_____
_____
_____
_____
_____

Notes: (Gun, gear, your performance)

_____
_____
_____
_____
_____
_____

Competition Handgun Training Logbook

Session/Phase: *C (Specialty Skills)*   Date: _____

Before you begin remember:

- ➢ Quality is the key to success.
- ➢ Push yourself to the next level, but pay attention to performing proper repetitions.

Gun/Gear (IDPA, USPSA, Etc.):			
Dry Fire Drill		*Beginning MTTS PAR Time*	*Ending MTTS PAR Time*
Draw and Transfer			
Reload and Transfer			
Target Acquisitions			
Pick up and Load			
Draw to Alternate Position			

Today's goal statement: (Where I want to go)

_____
_____
_____
_____
_____
_____

Notes: (Gun, gear, your performance)

_____
_____
_____
_____
_____
_____

Competition Handgun Training Logbook

Session/Phase: *A- (Drawing Skills)*   Date: _____

Before you begin remember:

- ➢ Quality is the key to success.
- ➢ Push yourself to the next level, but pay attention to performing proper repetitions.

Gun/Gear (IDPA, USPSA, Etc.):			
Dry Fire Drill		*Beginning MTTS PAR Time*	*Ending MTTS PAR Time*
Stationary Draw Hands Relaxed			
Stationary Draw Wrists Above Shoulders			
Stationary Draw Barricade			
Pivoting Draw			
Stepping Draw			
Table Draw			

Today's goal statement: (Where I want to go)

_____
_____
_____
_____
_____

Notes: (Gun, gear, your performance)

_____
_____
_____
_____
_____
_____

Competition Handgun Training Logbook

Session/Phase: *B (Reloading Skills)*   Date: _____

Before you begin remember:

- ➢ Quality is the key to success.
- ➢ Push yourself to the next level, but pay attention to performing proper repetitions.

Gun/Gear (IDPA, USPSA, Etc.):			
Dry Fire Drill		*Beginning MTTS PAR Time*	*Ending MTTS PAR Time*
Stationary Reload			
Stepping Reload			
Swinging Reload			
Table Reload			
IDPA Reload (reload with retention) **			
IDPA Reload (slidelock)**			

** IDPA Reloads only for those training in that sport

Today's goal statement: (Where I want to go)

_____
_____
_____
_____
_____

Notes: (Gun, gear, your performance)

_____
_____
_____
_____
_____
_____

Competition Handgun Training Logbook

Session/Phase: *A- (Drawing Skills)*   Date: _____

Before you begin remember:

- ➢ Quality is the key to success.
- ➢ Push yourself to the next level, but pay attention to performing proper repetitions.

Gun/Gear (IDPA, USPSA, Etc.):			
Dry Fire Drill		*Beginning MTTS PAR Time*	*Ending MTTS PAR Time*
Stationary Draw Hands Relaxed			
Stationary Draw Wrists Above Shoulders			
Stationary Draw Barricade			
Pivoting Draw			
Stepping Draw			
Table Draw			

Today's goal statement: (Where I want to go)

_____
_____
_____
_____
_____

Notes: (Gun, gear, your performance)

_____
_____
_____
_____
_____
_____

Competition Handgun Training Logbook

Session/Phase: *B (Reloading Skills)*   Date: _____

Before you begin remember:

- ➢ Quality is the key to success.
- ➢ Push yourself to the next level, but pay attention to performing proper repetitions.

Gun/Gear (IDPA, USPSA, Etc.):			
Dry Fire Drill		*Beginning MTTS PAR Time*	*Ending MTTS PAR Time*
Stationary Reload			
Stepping Reload			
Swinging Reload			
Table Reload			
IDPA Reload (reload with retention) **			
IDPA Reload (slidelock)**			

** *IDPA Reloads only for those training in that sport*

Today's goal statement: (Where I want to go)

_____
_____
_____
_____
_____

Notes: (Gun, gear, your performance)

_____
_____
_____
_____
_____

Competition Handgun Training Logbook

Session/Phase: *C (Specialty Skills)*   Date: _____

Before you begin remember:

- ➤ Quality is the key to success.
- ➤ Push yourself to the next level, but pay attention to performing proper repetitions.

Gun/Gear (IDPA, USPSA, Etc.):			
Dry Fire Drill		*Beginning MTTS PAR Time*	*Ending MTTS PAR Time*
Draw and Transfer			
Reload and Transfer			
Target Acquisitions			
Pick up and Load			
Draw to Alternate Position			

Today's goal statement: (Where I want to go)

_____
_____
_____
_____
_____

Notes: (Gun, gear, your performance)

_____
_____
_____
_____
_____
_____
_____

Competition Handgun Training Logbook

Session/Phase: *A- (Drawing Skills)*   Date: _____

Before you begin remember:

- ➢ Quality is the key to success.
- ➢ Push yourself to the next level, but pay attention to performing proper repetitions.

Gun/Gear (IDPA, USPSA, Etc.):			
Dry Fire Drill		*Beginning MTTS PAR Time*	*Ending MTTS PAR Time*
Stationary Draw Hands Relaxed			
Stationary Draw Wrists Above Shoulders			
Stationary Draw Barricade			
Pivoting Draw			
Stepping Draw			
Table Draw			

Today's goal statement: (Where I want to go)

_____

_____

_____

_____

_____

Notes: (Gun, gear, your performance)

_____

_____

_____

_____

_____

_____

Competition Handgun Training Logbook

Session/Phase: *B (Reloading Skills)*   Date: _____

Before you begin remember:

- ➢ Quality is the key to success.
- ➢ Push yourself to the next level, but pay attention to performing proper repetitions.

Gun/Gear (IDPA, USPSA, Etc.):			
Dry Fire Drill		*Beginning MTTS PAR Time*	*Ending MTTS PAR Time*
Stationary Reload			
Stepping Reload			
Swinging Reload			
Table Reload			
IDPA Reload (reload with retention) **			
IDPA Reload (slidelock)**			
** *IDPA Reloads only for those training in that sport*			

Today's goal statement: (Where I want to go)

_____

_____

_____

_____

_____

Notes: (Gun, gear, your performance)

_____

_____

_____

_____

_____

_____

Competition Handgun Training Logbook

Session/Phase: *A- (Drawing Skills)*   Date: _____

Before you begin remember:

- ➢ Quality is the key to success.
- ➢ Push yourself to the next level, but pay attention to performing proper repetitions.

Gun/Gear (IDPA, USPSA, Etc.):			
Dry Fire Drill		*Beginning MTTS PAR Time*	*Ending MTTS PAR Time*
Stationary Draw Hands Relaxed			
Stationary Draw Wrists Above Shoulders			
Stationary Draw Barricade			
Pivoting Draw			
Stepping Draw			
Table Draw			

Today's goal statement: (Where I want to go)

_____
_____
_____
_____
_____

Notes: (Gun, gear, your performance)

_____
_____
_____
_____
_____
_____

Session/Phase: B *(Reloading Skills)*   Date: _____

Before you begin remember:

- ➤ Quality is the key to success.
- ➤ Push yourself to the next level, but pay attention to performing proper repetitions.

Gun/Gear (IDPA, USPSA, Etc.):			
Dry Fire Drill		*Beginning MTTS PAR Time*	*Ending MTTS PAR Time*
Stationary Reload			
Stepping Reload			
Swinging Reload			
Table Reload			
IDPA Reload (reload with retention) **			
IDPA Reload (slidelock)**			
*** IDPA Reloads only for those training in that sport*			

Today's goal statement: (Where I want to go)

_____
_____
_____
_____
_____

Notes: (Gun, gear, your performance)

_____
_____
_____
_____
_____
_____

Competition Handgun Training Logbook

Session/Phase: *C (Specialty Skills)*   Date: _____

Before you begin remember:

- ➢ Quality is the key to success.
- ➢ Push yourself to the next level, but pay attention to performing proper repetitions.

Gun/Gear (IDPA, USPSA, Etc.):			
Dry Fire Drill		*Beginning MTTS PAR Time*	*Ending MTTS PAR Time*
Draw and Transfer			
Reload and Transfer			
Target Acquisitions			
Pick up and Load			
Draw to Alternate Position			

Today's goal statement: (Where I want to go)

_____
_____
_____
_____
_____

Notes: (Gun, gear, your performance)

_____
_____
_____
_____
_____

Competition Handgun Training Logbook

Session/Phase: *A- (Drawing Skills)*   Date: _____

Before you begin remember:

- ➢ Quality is the key to success.
- ➢ Push yourself to the next level, but pay attention to performing proper repetitions.

Gun/Gear (IDPA, USPSA, Etc.):			
Dry Fire Drill		*Beginning MTTS PAR Time*	*Ending MTTS PAR Time*
Stationary Draw Hands Relaxed			
Stationary Draw Wrists Above Shoulders			
Stationary Draw Barricade			
Pivoting Draw			
Stepping Draw			
Table Draw			

Today's goal statement: (Where I want to go)

_____
_____
_____
_____
_____

Notes: (Gun, gear, your performance)

_____
_____
_____
_____
_____
_____

Competition Handgun Training Logbook

Session/Phase: *B (Reloading Skills)*   Date: _____

Before you begin remember:

- ➢ Quality is the key to success.
- ➢ Push yourself to the next level, but pay attention to performing proper repetitions.

Gun/Gear (IDPA, USPSA, Etc.):			
Dry Fire Drill		**Beginning MTTS PAR Time**	**Ending MTTS PAR Time**
Stationary Reload			
Stepping Reload			
Swinging Reload			
Table Reload			
IDPA Reload (reload with retention) **			
IDPA Reload (slidelock)**			
** IDPA Reloads only for those training in that sport			

Today's goal statement: (Where I want to go)

_____
_____
_____
_____
_____

Notes: (Gun, gear, your performance)

_____
_____
_____
_____
_____
_____
_____

Competition Handgun Training Logbook

Session/Phase: *A- (Drawing Skills)*   Date: _____

Before you begin remember:

- ➢ Quality is the key to success.
- ➢ Push yourself to the next level, but pay attention to performing proper repetitions.

Gun/Gear (IDPA, USPSA, Etc.):			
Dry Fire Drill		*Beginning MTTS PAR Time*	*Ending MTTS PAR Time*
Stationary Draw Hands Relaxed			
Stationary Draw Wrists Above Shoulders			
Stationary Draw Barricade			
Pivoting Draw			
Stepping Draw			
Table Draw			

Today's goal statement: (Where I want to go)

_____
_____
_____
_____
_____

Notes: (Gun, gear, your performance)

_____
_____
_____
_____
_____
_____

Competition Handgun Training Logbook

Session/Phase: *B (Reloading Skills)*   Date: _____

Before you begin remember:

- ➢ Quality is the key to success.
- ➢ Push yourself to the next level, but pay attention to performing proper repetitions.

Gun/Gear (IDPA, USPSA, Etc.):			
Dry Fire Drill		*Beginning MTTS PAR Time*	*Ending MTTS PAR Time*
Stationary Reload			
Stepping Reload			
Swinging Reload			
Table Reload			
IDPA Reload (reload with retention) **			
IDPA Reload (slidelock)**			
** *IDPA Reloads only for those training in that sport*			

Today's goal statement: (Where I want to go)

_____

_____

_____

_____

_____

Notes: (Gun, gear, your performance)

_____

_____

_____

_____

_____

_____

Competition Handgun Training Logbook

Session/Phase: *C (Specialty Skills)*   Date: _____

Before you begin remember:

- ➢ Quality is the key to success.
- ➢ Push yourself to the next level, but pay attention to performing proper repetitions.

Gun/Gear (IDPA, USPSA, Etc.):			
Dry Fire Drill		*Beginning MTTS PAR Time*	*Ending MTTS PAR Time*
Draw and Transfer			
Reload and Transfer			
Target Acquisitions			
Pick up and Load			
Draw to Alternate Position			

Today's goal statement: (Where I want to go)

_____
_____
_____
_____
_____

Notes: (Gun, gear, your performance)

_____
_____
_____
_____
_____
_____

Session/Phase: *A- (Drawing Skills)*   Date: _____

Before you begin remember:

> - Quality is the key to success.
> - Push yourself to the next level, but pay attention to performing proper repetitions.

Gun/Gear (IDPA, USPSA, Etc.):			
Dry Fire Drill		*Beginning MTTS PAR Time*	*Ending MTTS PAR Time*
Stationary Draw Hands Relaxed			
Stationary Draw Wrists Above Shoulders			
Stationary Draw Barricade			
Pivoting Draw			
Stepping Draw			
Table Draw			

Today's goal statement: (Where I want to go)

_____
_____
_____
_____
_____

Notes: (Gun, gear, your performance)

_____
_____
_____
_____
_____
_____

Competition Handgun Training Logbook

Session/Phase: *B (Reloading Skills)*   Date: _____

Before you begin remember:

- ➢ Quality is the key to success.
- ➢ Push yourself to the next level, but pay attention to performing proper repetitions.

Gun/Gear (IDPA, USPSA, Etc.):			
Dry Fire Drill		*Beginning MTTS PAR Time*	*Ending MTTS PAR Time*
Stationary Reload			
Stepping Reload			
Swinging Reload			
Table Reload			
IDPA Reload (reload with retention) **			
IDPA Reload (slidelock)**			
*** IDPA Reloads only for those training in that sport*			

Today's goal statement: (Where I want to go)

_____
_____
_____
_____
_____

Notes: (Gun, gear, your performance)

_____
_____
_____
_____
_____

Competition Handgun Training Logbook

Session/Phase: *A- (Drawing Skills)*   Date: _____

Before you begin remember:

- ➤ Quality is the key to success.
- ➤ Push yourself to the next level, but pay attention to performing proper repetitions.

Gun/Gear (IDPA, USPSA, Etc.):			
Dry Fire Drill		*Beginning MTTS PAR Time*	*Ending MTTS PAR Time*
Stationary Draw Hands Relaxed			
Stationary Draw Wrists Above Shoulders			
Stationary Draw Barricade			
Pivoting Draw			
Stepping Draw			
Table Draw			

Today's goal statement: (Where I want to go)

_____
_____
_____
_____
_____

Notes: (Gun, gear, your performance)

_____
_____
_____
_____
_____
_____

Competition Handgun Training Logbook

Session/Phase: *B (Reloading Skills)*   Date: _____

Before you begin remember:

- ➢ Quality is the key to success.
- ➢ Push yourself to the next level, but pay attention to performing proper repetitions.

Gun/Gear (IDPA, USPSA, Etc.):			
Dry Fire Drill		*Beginning MTTS PAR Time*	*Ending MTTS PAR Time*
Stationary Reload			
Stepping Reload			
Swinging Reload			
Table Reload			
IDPA Reload (reload with retention) **			
IDPA Reload (slidelock)**			
** *IDPA Reloads only for those training in that sport*			

Today's goal statement: (Where I want to go)

_____

_____

_____

_____

_____

Notes: (Gun, gear, your performance)

_____

_____

_____

_____

_____

_____

Competition Handgun Training Logbook

Session/Phase: *C (Specialty Skills)*   Date: _____

Before you begin remember:

> - Quality is the key to success.
> - Push yourself to the next level, but pay attention to performing proper repetitions.

Gun/Gear (IDPA, USPSA, Etc.):			
Dry Fire Drill		*Beginning MTTS PAR Time*	*Ending MTTS PAR Time*
Draw and Transfer			
Reload and Transfer			
Target Acquisitions			
Pick up and Load			
Draw to Alternate Position			

Today's goal statement: (Where I want to go)

_____
_____
_____
_____
_____

Notes: (Gun, gear, your performance)

_____
_____
_____
_____
_____
_____

Competition Handgun Training Logbook

Session/Phase: *A- (Drawing Skills)*   Date: _____

Before you begin remember:

> - Quality is the key to success.
> - Push yourself to the next level, but pay attention to performing proper repetitions.

Gun/Gear (IDPA, USPSA, Etc.):			
Dry Fire Drill		*Beginning MTTS PAR Time*	*Ending MTTS PAR Time*
Stationary Draw Hands Relaxed			
Stationary Draw Wrists Above Shoulders			
Stationary Draw Barricade			
Pivoting Draw			
Stepping Draw			
Table Draw			

Today's goal statement: (Where I want to go)

_____
_____
_____
_____
_____

Notes: (Gun, gear, your performance)

_____
_____
_____
_____
_____

Competition Handgun Training Logbook

Session/Phase: *B (Reloading Skills)*   Date: _____

Before you begin remember:

> ➢ Quality is the key to success.
> ➢ Push yourself to the next level, but pay attention to performing proper repetitions.

Gun/Gear (IDPA, USPSA, Etc.):			
Dry Fire Drill		*Beginning MTTS PAR Time*	*Ending MTTS PAR Time*
Stationary Reload			
Stepping Reload			
Swinging Reload			
Table Reload			
IDPA Reload (reload with retention) **			
IDPA Reload (slidelock)**			

** *IDPA Reloads only for those training in that sport*

Today's goal statement: (Where I want to go)

_____
_____
_____
_____
_____

Notes: (Gun, gear, your performance)

_____
_____
_____
_____
_____
_____
_____

Competition Handgun Training Logbook

Session/Phase: *A- (Drawing Skills)*   Date: _____

Before you begin remember:

- ➢ Quality is the key to success.
- ➢ Push yourself to the next level, but pay attention to performing proper repetitions.

Gun/Gear (IDPA, USPSA, Etc.):			
Dry Fire Drill		*Beginning MTTS PAR Time*	*Ending MTTS PAR Time*
Stationary Draw Hands Relaxed			
Stationary Draw Wrists Above Shoulders			
Stationary Draw Barricade			
Pivoting Draw			
Stepping Draw			
Table Draw			

Today's goal statement: (Where I want to go)

_____
_____
_____
_____
_____
_____

Notes: (Gun, gear, your performance)

_____
_____
_____
_____
_____
_____
_____

Competition Handgun Training Logbook

Session/Phase: *B (Reloading Skills)*   Date: _____

Before you begin remember:

- ➢ Quality is the key to success.
- ➢ Push yourself to the next level, but pay attention to performing proper repetitions.

Gun/Gear (IDPA, USPSA, Etc.):			
Dry Fire Drill		*Beginning MTTS PAR Time*	*Ending MTTS PAR Time*
Stationary Reload			
Stepping Reload			
Swinging Reload			
Table Reload			
IDPA Reload (reload with retention) **			
IDPA Reload (slidelock)**			

*** IDPA Reloads only for those training in that sport*

Today's goal statement: (Where I want to go)

_____
_____
_____
_____
_____

Notes: (Gun, gear, your performance)

_____
_____
_____
_____
_____
_____

Competition Handgun Training Logbook

Session/Phase: *C (Specialty Skills)*   Date: _____

Before you begin remember:

- ➢ Quality is the key to success.
- ➢ Push yourself to the next level, but pay attention to performing proper repetitions.

Gun/Gear (IDPA, USPSA, Etc.):		
Dry Fire Drill	***Beginning MTTS PAR Time***	***Ending MTTS PAR Time***
Draw and Transfer		
Reload and Transfer		
Target Acquisitions		
Pick up and Load		
Draw to Alternate Position		

Today's goal statement: (Where I want to go)

_____
_____
_____
_____
_____

Notes: (Gun, gear, your performance)

_____
_____
_____
_____
_____
_____

Live Fire Training Session Logs

"When shooting is simplified, all that exists is the firing cycle. Attempt to improve it during each session!"

Competition Handgun Training Logbook

Instructions: These training session log sheets are general in design and will allow you to record your training sessions, and all critical and relevant information. Each section has a specific purpose, and here are some guidelines for each section:

- **General Details.** This section should be self-explanatory. It is formatted so you can quickly jot down the details that will be important to you later on. Circle the appropriate answers, or write in the details.
- **Drill.** List the name of the drill you did here.
- **Times.** I have placed 10 blocks in a table format for you to list the times on 10 repetitions of whatever drill you did.
- **Points.** You can list this each time you shoot the drill (if you want to walk down and score the target), or you can list N/A here and count the total points after you are done with your 10 training sets. (FYI, a "set" is defined as doing the drill one time)
- **Totals.** List the total time and points here. I use this as a general measurement tool so I can figure out one hit factor for the entire drill. If you choose not to do this then use the space for whatever purpose you want!
- **Key Notes.** List anything else that stood out about the drill here. Try to think in terms of what you need to improve upon because of a weakness, so you can try to correct that item during your next training session.

Don't forget:

- Go through your *Focus Breath* and *Success Visualization Video*
- Review your *Performance Statement* and use it before repetitions
- Review your *Self Image Booster*
- Stay mentally connected

As a reminder, during each Phase, you will be following one of three different daily training plans each time you train. They are as follows:

- **A – Fundamental Skills-** *This session is designed to work your fundamental firing cycle skills.*

> ***B – Movement Skills-*** *This session focuses elements of the firing cycle, while moving. This session teaches you how to patiently wait for the sights to settle before firing the gun.*

> ***C – Specialty Skills-*** *This session focuses on the specialty skills we use in USPSA/IDPA.*

An overview of the drills contained in each session during **PHASE ONE:**

Session	Session A (Fundamentals)	RDS	Session B (Movement)	RDS	Session C (Specialty)	RDS
Drill's	ALL SESSIONS WILL BEGIN WITH THE FIVE ROUND WARM UP DRILL					
	Extending (toward) Prep and Press	40	Pivoting Draw Drill/Varied Target Area (clock drill)	48	Strong and Support Hand Transfer	60
	Horizontal (L-R) Prep and Press	45	Moving Draw/Varied Target Area (clock drill)	48	Draw, Reload and Transfer	60
	Static Draw/Varied Target Area	40	Shooting and Moving, Forward and Backward	120	Multi-Port Drill	80
	Static Reload/Varied Target Area	48				
	Long Range Challenge	60				
Total Rounds	233		216		200	

*An overview of the drills contained in each session during **PHASE TWO**:*

Session	Session A (fundamentals)	RDS	Session B (Movement)	RDS	Session C (Specialty)	RDS
Drill's	ALL SESSIONS WILL BEGIN WITH THE FIVE ROUND WARM UP DRILL					
	1 shot X-Drill	48	Short Movement into Position	50	Multi-Position Drill	40
	2 shot X-Drill	80	Long Movement into Position	60	Strong and Weak Hand X-Drill	80
	Acceleration/Dec-eleration	50	Shooting and Moving Multidirectional	90	Long Range Challenge II	60
	Multi-Hardcover Drill	40			Off Balance Shooting	40
Total Rounds	218		200		220	

*An overview of the drills contained in each session during **PHASE THREE**:*

Session	Session A (fundamentals)	RDS	Session B (Movement)	RDS	Session C (Specialty)	RDS
Drill's	ALL SESSIONS WILL BEGIN WITH THE FIVE ROUND WARM UP DRILL					
	1 shot X-Drill (phase 3)	48	Shooting and Moving, Aggressive Entry	60	Strong and Weak Hand X-Drill (phase 3)	40
	2 shot X-Drill (phase 3)	80	Shooting and Moving Multidirectional	90	Multi-Port Drill	40
	Barricade X-Drill	80	Moving Reload	60	Long Range Challenge III	60
	Multiple Distance with Reload	60			Target Acquisition	50
Total Rounds	268		210		190	

Competition Handgun Training Logbook

General Details

** DID YOU REVIEW YOUR LAST TRAINING LOG FOR KEY INFORMATION BEFORE BEGINNING?? **

Training Phase: **1 Session A**   Date: _____   Weather: Sunny Cloudy Rain Snow Windy Temp: _____

Gun: _____ Problems? Yes - No   Ammo: _____ Problems? Yes - No

Mental Routine: Combat (focus) Breath? Yes – No   Active Visualization? Yes - No   Passive Visualization? Yes - No

---

*Record your average times, and your best times. Constantly strive to push harder, while maintaining control. Note your best time. On smaller drills record averages and best times, but recording every repetition is not necessary.
**Maintain a speed where you can hit 90% accuracy in the combat effective zone with NO misses. Note where you lost control.

Drill 1: Extending (toward) Prep and Press — Best Time

Times										

Key Notes:

Drill 2: Horizontal (L-R) Prep and Press — Best Time

Times										

Key Notes:

Drill 3: Static Draw/ Varied Target Area — Best Time

Times										

Key Notes:

Drill 4: Static Reload/Varied Target Area — Best Time

Key Notes:										

Key Notes:

Copyright 2013, All rights reserved   www.shooting-performance.com

Competition Handgun Training Logbook

Drill 5: Long Range Challenge											Best Time
Key Notes:											
Key Notes:											

Success Analysis: (What I did really well)

_____
_____
_____
_____

Solution Analysis: (What I figured out or need to figure out)

_____
_____
_____
_____

General Notes: (Any additional notes on the training session)

_____
_____
_____
_____

Carry Over (write any **key notes** you want to stand out to you in your next training session on that future log page):

_____
_____
_____
_____

Competition Handgun Training Logbook

General Details

** DID YOU REVIEW YOUR LAST TRAINING LOG FOR KEY INFORMATION BEFORE BEGINNING?? **

Training Phase: **1 Session B**   Date: _____   Weather: Sunny   Cloudy   Rain   Snow   Windy   Temp: _____

Gun: _____ Problems? Yes - No   Ammo: _____ Problems? Yes - No

Mental Routine: Combat (focus) Breath? Yes – No   Active Visualization? Yes - No   Passive Visualization? Yes - No

*Record your average times, and your best times. Constantly strive to push harder, while maintaining control. Note your best time. On smaller drills record averages and best times, but recording every repetition is not necessary.
**Maintain a speed where you can hit 90% accuracy in the combat effective zone with NO misses. Note where you lost control.

Drill 1: Pivoting Draw Drill/ Varied Target Area (clock drill) — Best Time

Times										
Key Notes:										

Drill 2: Moving Draw/Varied Target Area (clock drill) — Best Time

Times										
Key Notes:										

Drill 3: Shooting and Moving, Forward and Backward — Best Time

Times										
Key Notes:										

Copyright 2013, All rights reserved   www.shooting-performance.com

Competition Handgun Training Logbook

Drill 4 (extra work, shooters choice):											Best Time
Key Notes:											
Key Notes:											

Success Analysis: (What I did really well)

_____
_____
_____
_____

Solution Analysis: (What I figured out or need to figure out)

_____
_____
_____
_____

General Notes: (Any additional notes on the training session)

_____
_____
_____
_____

Carry Over (write any **key notes** you want to stand out to you in your next training session on that future log page):

_____
_____
_____
_____

Competition Handgun Training Logbook

General Details

** DID YOU REVIEW YOUR LAST TRAINING LOG FOR KEY INFORMATION BEFORE BEGINNING?? **

Training Phase: **1 Session C**   Date: _____   Weather: Sunny Cloudy Rain Snow Windy Temp: _____

Gun: _____ Problems? Yes - No   Ammo: _____ Problems? Yes - No

Mental Routine: Combat (focus) Breath? Yes – No   Active Visualization? Yes - No   Passive Visualization? Yes - No

*Record your average times, and your best times. Constantly strive to push harder, while maintaining control. Note your best time. On smaller drills record averages and best times, but recording every repetition is not necessary.
**Maintain a speed where you can hit 90% accuracy in the combat effective zone with NO misses. Note where you lost control.

Drill 1: Strong and Support Hand Transfer — Best Time

Times										

Key Notes:

Drill 2: Draw, Reload and Transfer — Best Time

Times										

Key Notes:

Drill 3: Multi-Port Drill — Best Time

Times										

Key Notes:

Copyright 2013, All rights reserved   www.shooting-performance.com

Competition Handgun Training Logbook

Drill 4 (extra work, shooters choice):										Best Time
Key Notes:										
Key Notes:										

Success Analysis: (What I did really well)

_____
_____
_____
_____

Solution Analysis: (What I figured out or need to figure out)

_____
_____
_____
_____

General Notes: (Any additional notes on the training session)

_____
_____
_____
_____

Carry Over (write any **key notes** you want to stand out to you in your next training session on that future log page):

_____
_____
_____
_____

Competition Handgun Training Logbook

General Details
** DID YOU REVIEW YOUR LAST TRAINING LOG FOR KEY INFORMATION BEFORE BEGINNING?? **
Training Phase: **1 Session A**   Date: _____   Weather: Sunny Cloudy Rain Snow Windy Temp: _____
Gun: _____ Problems? Yes - No   Ammo: _____ Problems? Yes - No
Mental Routine: Combat (focus) Breath? Yes – No   Active Visualization? Yes - No   Passive Visualization? Yes - No

*Record your average times, and your best times. Constantly strive to push harder, while maintaining control. Note your best time. On smaller drills record averages and best times, but recording every repetition is not necessary.
**Maintain a speed where you can hit 90% accuracy in the combat effective zone with NO misses. Note where you lost control.

Drill 1: Extending (toward) Prep and Press										Best Time
Times										
Key Notes:										

Drill 2: Horizontal (L-R) Prep and Press										Best Time
Times										
Key Notes:										

Drill 3: Static Draw/ Varied Target Area										Best Time
Times										
Key Notes:										

Drill 4: Static Reload/Varied Target Area										Best Time
Key Notes:										
Key Notes:										

Copyright 2013, All rights reserved   www.shooting-performance.com

Competition Handgun Training Logbook

Drill 5: Long Range Challenge											Best Time
Key Notes:											
Key Notes:											

Success Analysis: (What I did really well)
_____
_____
_____
_____

Solution Analysis: (What I figured out or need to figure out)
_____
_____
_____
_____

General Notes: (Any additional notes on the training session)
_____
_____
_____
_____

Carry Over (write any **key notes** you want to stand out to you in your next training session on that future log page):
_____
_____
_____
_____

Competition Handgun Training Logbook

General Details

** DID YOU REVIEW YOUR LAST TRAINING LOG FOR KEY INFORMATION BEFORE BEGINNING?? **

Training Phase: **1 Session B**   Date: _____   Weather: Sunny Cloudy Rain Snow Windy Temp: _____

Gun: _____ Problems? Yes - No Ammo: _____ Problems? Yes - No

Mental Routine: Combat (focus) Breath? Yes – No   Active Visualization? Yes - No   Passive Visualization? Yes - No

*Record your average times, and your best times. Constantly strive to push harder, while maintaining control. Note your best time. On smaller drills record averages and best times, but recording every repetition is not necessary.
**Maintain a speed where you can hit 90% accuracy in the combat effective zone with NO misses. Note where you lost control.

Drill 1: Pivoting Draw Drill/ Varied Target Area (clock drill)										Best Time
Times										
Key Notes:										

Drill 2: Moving Draw/Varied Target Area (clock drill)										Best Time
Times										
Key Notes:										

Drill 3: Shooting and Moving, Forward and Backward										Best Time
Times										
Key Notes:										

Competition Handgun Training Logbook

Drill 4 (extra work, shooters choice):											Best Time
Key Notes:											
Key Notes:											

Success Analysis: (What I did really well)

_____
_____
_____
_____

Solution Analysis: (What I figured out or need to figure out)

_____
_____
_____
_____

General Notes: (Any additional notes on the training session)

_____
_____
_____
_____

Carry Over (write any **key notes** you want to stand out to you in your next training session on that future log page):

_____
_____
_____
_____

Competition Handgun Training Logbook

General Details

** DID YOU REVIEW YOUR LAST TRAINING LOG FOR KEY INFORMATION BEFORE BEGINNING?? **

Training Phase: **1 Session C**   Date: _____   Weather: Sunny Cloudy Rain Snow Windy Temp: _____

Gun: _____ Problems? Yes - No   Ammo: _____ Problems? Yes - No

Mental Routine: Combat (focus) Breath? Yes – No   Active Visualization? Yes - No   Passive Visualization? Yes - No

*Record your average times, and your best times. Constantly strive to push harder, while maintaining control. Note your best time. On smaller drills record averages and best times, but recording every repetition is not necessary.
**Maintain a speed where you can hit 90% accuracy in the combat effective zone with NO misses. Note where you lost control.

Drill 1: Strong and Support Hand Transfer											Best Time
Times											
Key Notes:											

Drill 2: Draw, Reload and Transfer											Best Time
Times											
Key Notes:											

Drill 3: Multi-Port Drill											Best Time
Times											
Key Notes:											

Competition Handgun Training Logbook

Drill 4 (extra work, shooters choice):										Best Time
Key Notes:										
Key Notes:										

Success Analysis: (What I did really well)

_____
_____
_____
_____

Solution Analysis: (What I figured out or need to figure out)

_____
_____
_____
_____

General Notes: (Any additional notes on the training session)

_____
_____
_____
_____

Carry Over (write any **key notes** you want to stand out to you in your next training session on that future log page):

_____
_____
_____
_____

Competition Handgun Training Logbook

General Details

** DID YOU REVIEW YOUR LAST TRAINING LOG FOR KEY INFORMATION BEFORE BEGINNING?? **

Training Phase: **1 Session A**   Date: _____   Weather: Sunny Cloudy Rain Snow Windy   Temp: _____

Gun: _____ Problems? Yes - No   Ammo: _____ Problems? Yes - No

Mental Routine: Combat (focus) Breath? Yes – No   Active Visualization? Yes - No   Passive Visualization? Yes - No

---

*Record your average times, and your best times. Constantly strive to push harder, while maintaining control. Note your best time. On smaller drills record averages and best times, but recording every repetition is not necessary.
**Maintain a speed where you can hit 90% accuracy in the combat effective zone with NO misses. Note where you lost control.

Drill 1: Extending (toward) Prep and Press										Best Time
Times										
Key Notes:										

Drill 2: Horizontal (L-R) Prep and Press										Best Time
Times										
Key Notes:										

Drill 3: Static Draw/ Varied Target Area										Best Time
Times										
Key Notes:										

Drill 4: Static Reload/Varied Target Area										Best Time
Key Notes:										
Key Notes:										

Copyright 2013, All rights reserved   www.shooting-performance.com

Competition Handgun Training Logbook

Drill 5: Long Range Challenge										Best Time
Key Notes:										
Key Notes:										

Success Analysis: (What I did really well)

_____
_____
_____
_____

Solution Analysis: (What I figured out or need to figure out)

_____
_____
_____
_____

General Notes: (Any additional notes on the training session)

_____
_____
_____
_____

Carry Over (write any **key notes** you want to stand out to you in your next training session on that future log page):

_____
_____
_____
_____

Competition Handgun Training Logbook

General Details

** DID YOU REVIEW YOUR LAST TRAINING LOG FOR KEY INFORMATION BEFORE BEGINNING?? **

Training Phase: **1 Session B**   Date: _____   Weather: Sunny Cloudy Rain Snow Windy Temp: _____

Gun: _____ Problems? Yes - No   Ammo: _____ Problems? Yes - No

Mental Routine: Combat (focus) Breath? Yes – No   Active Visualization? Yes - No   Passive Visualization? Yes - No

---

*Record your average times, and your best times. Constantly strive to push harder, while maintaining control. Note your best time. On smaller drills record averages and best times, but recording every repetition is not necessary.
**Maintain a speed where you can hit 90% accuracy in the combat effective zone with NO misses. Note where you lost control.

Drill 1: Pivoting Draw Drill/ Varied Target Area (clock drill)   Best Time

Times										

Key Notes:

Drill 2: Moving Draw/Varied Target Area (clock drill)   Best Time

Times										

Key Notes:

Drill 3: Shooting and Moving, Forward and Backward   Best Time

Times										

Key Notes:

Copyright 2013, All rights reserved   www.shooting-performance.com

Competition Handgun Training Logbook

Drill 4 (extra work, shooters choice):										Best Time
Key Notes:										
Key Notes:										

Success Analysis: (What I did really well)

_____
_____
_____
_____

Solution Analysis: (What I figured out or need to figure out)

_____
_____
_____
_____

General Notes: (Any additional notes on the training session)

_____
_____
_____
_____
_____

Carry Over (write any **key notes** you want to stand out to you in your next training session on that future log page):

_____
_____
_____
_____

Competition Handgun Training Logbook

General Details

** DID YOU REVIEW YOUR LAST TRAINING LOG FOR KEY INFORMATION BEFORE BEGINNING?? **

Training Phase: **1 Session C**   Date: _____   Weather: Sunny Cloudy Rain Snow Windy Temp: _____

Gun: _____ Problems? Yes - No   Ammo: _____ Problems? Yes - No

Mental Routine: Combat (focus) Breath? Yes – No   Active Visualization? Yes - No   Passive Visualization? Yes - No

*Record your average times, and your best times. Constantly strive to push harder, while maintaining control. Note your best time. On smaller drills record averages and best times, but recording every repetition is not necessary.
**Maintain a speed where you can hit 90% accuracy in the combat effective zone with NO misses. Note where you lost control.

Drill 1: Strong and Support Hand Transfer | Best Time

Times										

Key Notes:

Drill 2: Draw, Reload and Transfer | Best Time

Times										

Key Notes:

Drill 3: Multi-Port Drill | Best Time

Times										

Key Notes:

Competition Handgun Training Logbook

Drill 4 (extra work, shooters choice):											Best Time
Key Notes:											
Key Notes:											

Success Analysis: (What I did really well)

_____
_____
_____
_____

Solution Analysis: (What I figured out or need to figure out)

_____
_____
_____
_____

General Notes: (Any additional notes on the training session)

_____
_____
_____
_____

Carry Over (write any **key notes** you want to stand out to you in your next training session on that future log page):

_____
_____
_____
_____

Competition Handgun Training Logbook

General Details

** DID YOU REVIEW YOUR LAST TRAINING LOG FOR KEY INFORMATION BEFORE BEGINNING?? **

Training Phase: **1 Session A**   Date: _____   Weather: Sunny Cloudy Rain Snow Windy   Temp: _____

Gun: _____ Problems? Yes - No   Ammo: _____ Problems? Yes - No

Mental Routine: Combat (focus) Breath? Yes – No   Active Visualization? Yes - No   Passive Visualization? Yes - No

*Record your average times, and your best times. Constantly strive to push harder, while maintaining control. Note your best time. On smaller drills record averages and best times, but recording every repetition is not necessary.
**Maintain a speed where you can hit 90% accuracy in the combat effective zone with NO misses. Note where you lost control.

Drill 1: Extending (toward) Prep and Press										Best Time
Times										
Key Notes:										

Drill 2: Horizontal (L-R) Prep and Press										Best Time
Times										
Key Notes:										

Drill 3: Static Draw/ Varied Target Area										Best Time
Times										
Key Notes:										

Drill 4: Static Reload/Varied Target Area										Best Time
Key Notes:										
Key Notes:										

Copyright 2013, All rights reserved   www.shooting-performance.com

Competition Handgun Training Logbook

Drill 5: Long Range Challenge										Best Time
Key Notes:										
Key Notes:										

Success Analysis: (What I did really well)

_____
_____
_____
_____

Solution Analysis: (What I figured out or need to figure out)

_____
_____
_____
_____

General Notes: (Any additional notes on the training session)

_____
_____
_____
_____

Carry Over (write any **key notes** you want to stand out to you in your next training session on that future log page):

_____
_____
_____
_____

Competition Handgun Training Logbook

General Details

** DID YOU REVIEW YOUR LAST TRAINING LOG FOR KEY INFORMATION BEFORE BEGINNING?? **

Training Phase: **1 Session B**   Date: _____   Weather: Sunny   Cloudy   Rain   Snow   Windy   Temp: _____

Gun: _____ Problems? Yes - No   Ammo: _____ Problems? Yes - No

Mental Routine: Combat (focus) Breath? Yes – No   Active Visualization? Yes - No   Passive Visualization? Yes - No

*Record your average times, and your best times. Constantly strive to push harder, while maintaining control. Note your best time. On smaller drills record averages and best times, but recording every repetition is not necessary.
**Maintain a speed where you can hit 90% accuracy in the combat effective zone with NO misses. Note where you lost control.

Drill 1: Pivoting Draw Drill/ Varied Target Area (clock drill)										Best Time
Times										
Key Notes:										

Drill 2: Moving Draw/Varied Target Area (clock drill)										Best Time
Times										
Key Notes:										

Drill 3: Shooting and Moving, Forward and Backward										Best Time
Times										
Key Notes:										

Copyright 2013, All rights reserved   www.shooting-performance.com

Competition Handgun Training Logbook

Drill 4 (extra work, shooters choice):										Best Time
Key Notes:										
Key Notes:										

Success Analysis: (What I did really well)

_____
_____
_____
_____

Solution Analysis: (What I figured out or need to figure out)

_____
_____
_____
_____

General Notes: (Any additional notes on the training session)

_____
_____
_____
_____
_____

Carry Over (write any **key notes** you want to stand out to you in your next training session on that future log page):

_____
_____
_____
_____

Competition Handgun Training Logbook

General Details

** DID YOU REVIEW YOUR LAST TRAINING LOG FOR KEY INFORMATION BEFORE BEGINNING?? **

Training Phase: **1 Session C**   Date: _____   Weather: Sunny Cloudy Rain Snow Windy Temp: _____

Gun: _____ Problems? Yes - No   Ammo: _____ Problems? Yes - No

Mental Routine: Combat (focus) Breath? Yes – No   Active Visualization? Yes - No   Passive Visualization? Yes - No

---

*Record your average times, and your best times. Constantly strive to push harder, while maintaining control. Note your best time. On smaller drills record averages and best times, but recording every repetition is not necessary.
**Maintain a speed where you can hit 90% accuracy in the combat effective zone with NO misses. Note where you lost control.

Drill 1: Strong and Support Hand Transfer										Best Time
Times										
Key Notes:										

Drill 2: Draw, Reload and Transfer										Best Time
Times										
Key Notes:										

Drill 3: Multi-Port Drill										Best Time
Times										
Key Notes:										

Competition Handgun Training Logbook

Drill 4 (extra work, shooters choice):										Best Time
Key Notes:										
Key Notes:										

Success Analysis: (What I did really well)
_____
_____
_____
_____

Solution Analysis: (What I figured out or need to figure out)
_____
_____
_____
_____

General Notes: (Any additional notes on the training session)
_____
_____
_____
_____

Carry Over (write any **key notes** you want to stand out to you in your next training session on that future log page):
_____
_____
_____
_____

Competition Handgun Training Logbook

General Details

** DID YOU REVIEW YOUR LAST TRAINING LOG FOR KEY INFORMATION BEFORE BEGINNING?? **

Training Phase: **1 Session A**   Date: _____   Weather: Sunny Cloudy Rain Snow Windy   Temp: _____

Gun: _____ Problems? Yes - No   Ammo: _____ Problems? Yes - No

Mental Routine: Combat (focus) Breath? Yes – No   Active Visualization? Yes - No   Passive Visualization? Yes - No

*Record your average times, and your best times. Constantly strive to push harder, while maintaining control. Note your best time. On smaller drills record averages and best times, but recording every repetition is not necessary.
**Maintain a speed where you can hit 90% accuracy in the combat effective zone with NO misses. Note where you lost control.

Drill 1: Extending (toward) Prep and Press										Best Time
Times										
Key Notes:										

Drill 2: Horizontal (L-R) Prep and Press										Best Time
Times										
Key Notes:										

Drill 3: Static Draw/ Varied Target Area										Best Time
Times										
Key Notes:										

Drill 4: Static Reload/Varied Target Area										Best Time
Key Notes:										
Key Notes:										

Copyright 2013, All rights reserved   www.shooting-performance.com

Competition Handgun Training Logbook

Drill 5: Long Range Challenge										Best Time
Key Notes:										
Key Notes:										

Success Analysis: (What I did really well)

_____
_____
_____
_____

Solution Analysis: (What I figured out or need to figure out)

_____
_____
_____
_____

General Notes: (Any additional notes on the training session)

_____
_____
_____
_____

Carry Over (write any **key notes** you want to stand out to you in your next training session on that future log page):

_____
_____
_____
_____

Competition Handgun Training Logbook

General Details

** DID YOU REVIEW YOUR LAST TRAINING LOG FOR KEY INFORMATION BEFORE BEGINNING?? **

Training Phase: **1 Session B**   Date: _____   Weather: Sunny   Cloudy   Rain   Snow   Windy   Temp: _____

Gun: _____ Problems? Yes - No   Ammo: _____ Problems? Yes - No

Mental Routine: Combat (focus) Breath? Yes – No   Active Visualization? Yes - No   Passive Visualization? Yes - No

*Record your average times, and your best times. Constantly strive to push harder, while maintaining control. Note your best time. On smaller drills record averages and best times, but recording every repetition is not necessary.
**Maintain a speed where you can hit 90% accuracy in the combat effective zone with NO misses. Note where you lost control.

Drill 1: Pivoting Draw Drill/ Varied Target Area (clock drill)											Best Time
Times											
Key Notes:											

Drill 2: Moving Draw/Varied Target Area (clock drill)											Best Time
Times											
Key Notes:											

Drill 3: Shooting and Moving, Forward and Backward											Best Time
Times											
Key Notes:											

Competition Handgun Training Logbook

Drill 4 (extra work, shooters choice):										Best Time
Key Notes:										
Key Notes:										

Success Analysis: (What I did really well)

_____
_____
_____
_____

Solution Analysis: (What I figured out or need to figure out)

_____
_____
_____
_____

General Notes: (Any additional notes on the training session)

_____
_____
_____
_____

Carry Over (write any **key notes** you want to stand out to you in your next training session on that future log page):

_____
_____
_____
_____

Competition Handgun Training Logbook

General Details

** DID YOU REVIEW YOUR LAST TRAINING LOG FOR KEY INFORMATION BEFORE BEGINNING?? **

Training Phase: **1 Session C**   Date: _____   Weather: Sunny Cloudy Rain Snow Windy Temp: _____

Gun: _____ Problems? Yes - No   Ammo: _____ Problems? Yes - No

Mental Routine: Combat (focus) Breath? Yes – No   Active Visualization? Yes - No   Passive Visualization? Yes - No

*Record your average times, and your best times. Constantly strive to push harder, while maintaining control. Note your best time. On smaller drills record averages and best times, but recording every repetition is not necessary.
**Maintain a speed where you can hit 90% accuracy in the combat effective zone with NO misses. Note where you lost control.

Drill 1: Strong and Support Hand Transfer										Best Time
Times										
Key Notes:										

Drill 2: Draw, Reload and Transfer										Best Time
Times										
Key Notes:										

Drill 3: Multi-Port Drill										Best Time
Times										
Key Notes:										

Competition Handgun Training Logbook

Drill 4 (extra work, shooters choice):										Best Time
Key Notes:										
Key Notes:										

Success Analysis: (What I did really well)

_____
_____
_____
_____

Solution Analysis: (What I figured out or need to figure out)

_____
_____
_____
_____

General Notes: (Any additional notes on the training session)

_____
_____
_____
_____

Carry Over (write any **key notes** you want to stand out to you in your next training session on that future log page):

_____
_____
_____
_____

You have completed **Phase One**! Accomplish the following before beginning Phase Two:

- Assess whether you are ready to begin Phase Two. If necessary, you may repeat some of the Phase One training sessions before continuing on.
- Rest and review. This is your chance to rest and take a week off from training. Review your Phase One notes and prepare yourself physically and mentally to begin the next session.

Phase One Notes:

_____
_____
_____
_____
_____
_____
_____
_____
_____
_____
_____
_____
_____
_____
_____

Begin Phase Two

Competition Handgun Training Logbook

General Details

** DID YOU REVIEW YOUR LAST TRAINING LOG FOR KEY INFORMATION BEFORE BEGINNING?? **

Training Phase: **2 Session A**   Date: _____   Weather: Sunny Cloudy Rain Snow Windy Temp: _____

Gun: _____ Problems? Yes - No   Ammo: _____ Problems? Yes - No

Mental Routine: Combat (focus) Breath? Yes – No   Active Visualization? Yes - No   Passive Visualization? Yes - No

*Record your average times, and your best times. Constantly strive to push harder, while maintaining control. Note your best time. On smaller drills record averages and best times, but recording every repetition is not necessary.
**Maintain a speed where you can hit 90% accuracy in the combat effective zone with NO misses. Note where you lost control.

Drill 1: 1 shot X-Drill | Best Time

Times										

Key Notes:

Drill 2: 2 shot X-Drill | Best Time

Times										

Key Notes:

Drill 3: Acceleration/Deceleration Drill | Best Time

Times										

Key Notes:

Drill 4: Multi-Hardcover Drill | Best Time

Key Notes:										

Key Notes:

Copyright 2013, All rights reserved   www.shooting-performance.com

Competition Handgun Training Logbook

Drill 5 (extra work, shooters choice):										Best Time
Key Notes:										
Key Notes:										

Success Analysis: (What I did really well)

_____
_____
_____
_____

Solution Analysis: (What I figured out or need to figure out)

_____
_____
_____
_____

General Notes: (Any additional notes on the training session)

_____
_____
_____
_____

Carry Over (write any **key notes** you want to stand out to you in your next training session on that future log page):

_____
_____
_____
_____

Competition Handgun Training Logbook

General Details

** DID YOU REVIEW YOUR LAST TRAINING LOG FOR KEY INFORMATION BEFORE BEGINNING?? **

Training Phase: **2 Session B**   Date: _____   Weather: Sunny Cloudy Rain Snow Windy Temp: _____

Gun: _____ Problems? Yes - No   Ammo: _____ Problems? Yes - No

Mental Routine: Combat (focus) Breath? Yes – No   Active Visualization? Yes - No   Passive Visualization? Yes - No

---

*Record your average times, and your best times. Constantly strive to push harder, while maintaining control. Note your best time. On smaller drills record averages and best times, but recording every repetition is not necessary.
**Maintain a speed where you can hit 90% accuracy in the combat effective zone with NO misses. Note where you lost control.

Drill 1: Short Movement into Position | Best Time

Times											

Key Notes:

Drill 2: Long Movement into Position | Best Time

Times											

Key Notes:

Drill 3: Shooting and Moving Multi-Directional | Best Time

Times											

Key Notes:

Competition Handgun Training Logbook

Drill 4 (extra work, shooters choice):										Best Time
Key Notes:										
Key Notes:										

Success Analysis: (What I did really well)
_____
_____
_____
_____

Solution Analysis: (What I figured out or need to figure out)
_____
_____
_____
_____

General Notes: (Any additional notes on the training session)
_____
_____
_____
_____

Carry Over (write any **key notes** you want to stand out to you in your next training session on that future log page):
_____
_____
_____
_____

Competition Handgun Training Logbook

General Details

** DID YOU REVIEW YOUR LAST TRAINING LOG FOR KEY INFORMATION BEFORE BEGINNING?? **

Training Phase: **2 Session C** Date: _____ Weather: Sunny Cloudy Rain Snow Windy Temp: _____

Gun: _____ Problems? Yes - No Ammo: _____ Problems? Yes - No

Mental Routine: Combat (focus) Breath? Yes – No Active Visualization? Yes - No Passive Visualization? Yes - No

*Record your average times, and your best times. Constantly strive to push harder, while maintaining control. Note your best time. On smaller drills record averages and best times, but recording every repetition is not necessary.
**Maintain a speed where you can hit 90% accuracy in the combat effective zone with NO misses. Note where you lost control.

Drill 1: Multi-Position Drill | Best Time

Times										
Key Notes:										

Drill 2: Strong and Weak Hand X-Drill | Best Time

Times										
Key Notes:										

Drill 3: Long Range Challenge II | Best Time

Times										
Key Notes:										

Competition Handgun Training Logbook

Drill 4: Off Balance Shooting											Best Time
Key Notes:											
Key Notes:											

Success Analysis: (What I did really well)

_____
_____
_____
_____

Solution Analysis: (What I figured out or need to figure out)

_____
_____
_____
_____

General Notes: (Any additional notes on the training session)

_____
_____
_____
_____

Carry Over (write any **key notes** you want to stand out to you in your next training session on that future log page):

_____
_____
_____
_____

Competition Handgun Training Logbook

General Details
** DID YOU REVIEW YOUR LAST TRAINING LOG FOR KEY INFORMATION BEFORE BEGINNING?? **

Training Phase: **2 Session A**   Date: _____   Weather: Sunny Cloudy Rain Snow Windy Temp: _____

Gun: _____ Problems? Yes - No   Ammo: _____ Problems? Yes - No

Mental Routine: Combat (focus) Breath? Yes – No   Active Visualization? Yes - No   Passive Visualization? Yes - No

*Record your average times, and your best times. Constantly strive to push harder, while maintaining control. Note your best time. On smaller drills record averages and best times, but recording every repetition is not necessary.
**Maintain a speed where you can hit 90% accuracy in the combat effective zone with NO misses. Note where you lost control.

Drill 1: 1 shot X-Drill   Best Time

Times										

Key Notes:

Drill 2: 2 shot X-Drill   Best Time

Times										

Key Notes:

Drill 3: Acceleration/Deceleration Drill   Best Time

Times										

Key Notes:

Drill 4: Multi-Hardcover Drill   Best Time

Key Notes:

Key Notes:

Copyright 2013, All rights reserved   www.shooting-performance.com

Competition Handgun Training Logbook

Drill 5 (extra work, shooters choice):										Best Time
Key Notes:										
Key Notes:										

Success Analysis: (What I did really well)

_____
_____
_____
_____

Solution Analysis: (What I figured out or need to figure out)

_____
_____
_____
_____

General Notes: (Any additional notes on the training session)

_____
_____
_____
_____

Carry Over (write any **key notes** you want to stand out to you in your next training session on that future log page):

_____
_____
_____
_____

Competition Handgun Training Logbook

General Details

** DID YOU REVIEW YOUR LAST TRAINING LOG FOR KEY INFORMATION BEFORE BEGINNING?? **

Training Phase: **2 Session B**   Date: _____   Weather: Sunny Cloudy Rain Snow Windy Temp: _____

Gun: _____ Problems? Yes - No   Ammo: _____ Problems? Yes - No

Mental Routine: Combat (focus) Breath? Yes – No   Active Visualization? Yes - No   Passive Visualization? Yes - No

---

*Record your average times, and your best times. Constantly strive to push harder, while maintaining control. Note your best time. On smaller drills record averages and best times, but recording every repetition is not necessary.
**Maintain a speed where you can hit 90% accuracy in the combat effective zone with NO misses. Note where you lost control.

Drill 1: Short Movement into Position										Best Time
Times										
Key Notes:										

Drill 2: Long Movement into Position										Best Time
Times										
Key Notes:										

Drill 3: Shooting and Moving Multi-Directional										Best Time
Times										
Key Notes:										

Competition Handgun Training Logbook

Drill 4 (extra work, shooters choice):										Best Time
Key Notes:										
Key Notes:										

Success Analysis: (What I did really well)

_____
_____
_____
_____

Solution Analysis: (What I figured out or need to figure out)

_____
_____
_____
_____

General Notes: (Any additional notes on the training session)

_____
_____
_____
_____

Carry Over (write any **key notes** you want to stand out to you in your next training session on that future log page):

_____
_____
_____
_____

Competition Handgun Training Logbook

General Details

** DID YOU REVIEW YOUR LAST TRAINING LOG FOR KEY INFORMATION BEFORE BEGINNING?? **

Training Phase: **2 Session C**   Date: _____   Weather: Sunny Cloudy Rain Snow Windy   Temp: _____

Gun: _____ Problems? Yes - No   Ammo: _____ Problems? Yes - No

Mental Routine: Combat (focus) Breath? Yes – No   Active Visualization? Yes - No   Passive Visualization? Yes - No

---

*Record your average times, and your best times. Constantly strive to push harder, while maintaining control. Note your best time. On smaller drills record averages and best times, but recording every repetition is not necessary.
**Maintain a speed where you can hit 90% accuracy in the combat effective zone with NO misses. Note where you lost control.

Drill 1: Multi-Position Drill   Best Time

Times										

Key Notes:

Drill 2: Strong and Weak Hand X-Drill   Best Time

Times										

Key Notes:

Drill 3: Long Range Challenge II   Best Time

Times										

Key Notes:

Competition Handgun Training Logbook

Drill 4: Off Balance Shooting										Best Time
Key Notes:										
Key Notes:										

Success Analysis: (What I did really well)

_____
_____
_____
_____

Solution Analysis: (What I figured out or need to figure out)

_____
_____
_____
_____

General Notes: (Any additional notes on the training session)

_____
_____
_____
_____

Carry Over (write any **key notes** you want to stand out to you in your next training session on that future log page):

_____
_____
_____
_____

Competition Handgun Training Logbook

General Details

** DID YOU REVIEW YOUR LAST TRAINING LOG FOR KEY INFORMATION BEFORE BEGINNING?? **

Training Phase: **2 Session A**   Date: _____   Weather: Sunny Cloudy Rain Snow Windy   Temp: _____

Gun: _____   Problems? Yes - No   Ammo: _____   Problems? Yes - No

Mental Routine: Combat (focus) Breath? Yes – No   Active Visualization? Yes - No   Passive Visualization? Yes - No

*Record your average times, and your best times. Constantly strive to push harder, while maintaining control. Note your best time. On smaller drills record averages and best times, but recording every repetition is not necessary.
**Maintain a speed where you can hit 90% accuracy in the combat effective zone with NO misses. Note where you lost control.

Drill 1: 1 shot X-Drill										Best Time
Times										
Key Notes:										

Drill 2: 2 shot X-Drill										Best Time
Times										
Key Notes:										

Drill 3: Acceleration/Deceleration Drill										Best Time
Times										
Key Notes:										

Drill 4: Multi-Hardcover Drill										Best Time
Key Notes:										
Key Notes:										

Competition Handgun Training Logbook

Drill 5 (extra work, shooters choice):										Best Time
Key Notes:										
Key Notes:										

Success Analysis: (What I did really well)

_____
_____
_____
_____

Solution Analysis: (What I figured out or need to figure out)

_____
_____
_____
_____

General Notes: (Any additional notes on the training session)

_____
_____
_____
_____

Carry Over (write any **key notes** you want to stand out to you in your next training session on that future log page):

_____
_____
_____
_____

Competition Handgun Training Logbook

General Details

** DID YOU REVIEW YOUR LAST TRAINING LOG FOR KEY INFORMATION BEFORE BEGINNING?? **

Training Phase: **2 Session B**   Date: _____   Weather: Sunny Cloudy Rain Snow Windy Temp: _____

Gun: _____ Problems? Yes - No   Ammo: _____ Problems? Yes - No

Mental Routine: Combat (focus) Breath? Yes – No   Active Visualization? Yes - No   Passive Visualization? Yes - No

*Record your average times, and your best times. Constantly strive to push harder, while maintaining control. Note your best time. On smaller drills record averages and best times, but recording every repetition is not necessary.
**Maintain a speed where you can hit 90% accuracy in the combat effective zone with NO misses. Note where you lost control.

Drill 1: Short Movement into Position — Best Time

Times											
Key Notes:											

Drill 2: Long Movement into Position — Best Time

Times											
Key Notes:											

Drill 3: Shooting and Moving Multi-Directional — Best Time

Times											
Key Notes:											

Competition Handgun Training Logbook

Drill 4 (extra work, shooters choice):											Best Time
Key Notes:											
Key Notes:											

Success Analysis: (What I did really well)
_____
_____
_____
_____

Solution Analysis: (What I figured out or need to figure out)
_____
_____
_____
_____

General Notes: (Any additional notes on the training session)
_____
_____
_____
_____

Carry Over (write any **key notes** you want to stand out to you in your next training session on that future log page):
_____
_____
_____
_____

Competition Handgun Training Logbook

General Details

** DID YOU REVIEW YOUR LAST TRAINING LOG FOR KEY INFORMATION BEFORE BEGINNING?? **

Training Phase: **2 Session C**   Date: _____   Weather: Sunny Cloudy Rain Snow Windy Temp: _____

Gun: _____ Problems? Yes - No   Ammo: _____ Problems? Yes - No

Mental Routine: Combat (focus) Breath? Yes – No   Active Visualization? Yes - No   Passive Visualization? Yes - No

---

*Record your average times, and your best times. Constantly strive to push harder, while maintaining control. Note your best time. On smaller drills record averages and best times, but recording every repetition is not necessary.
**Maintain a speed where you can hit 90% accuracy in the combat effective zone with NO misses. Note where you lost control.

Drill 1: Multi-Position Drill | Best Time

Times										

Key Notes:

Drill 2: Strong and Weak Hand X-Drill | Best Time

Times										

Key Notes:

Drill 3: Long Range Challenge II | Best Time

Times										

Key Notes:

Competition Handgun Training Logbook

Drill 4: Off Balance Shooting											Best Time
Key Notes:											
Key Notes:											

Success Analysis: (What I did really well)

_____
_____
_____
_____

Solution Analysis: (What I figured out or need to figure out)

_____
_____
_____
_____

General Notes: (Any additional notes on the training session)

_____
_____
_____
_____

Carry Over (write any **key notes** you want to stand out to you in your next training session on that future log page):

_____
_____
_____
_____

Competition Handgun Training Logbook

General Details

** DID YOU REVIEW YOUR LAST TRAINING LOG FOR KEY INFORMATION BEFORE BEGINNING?? **

Training Phase: **2 Session A**   Date: _____   Weather: Sunny Cloudy Rain Snow Windy Temp: _____

Gun: _____ Problems? Yes - No   Ammo: _____ Problems? Yes - No

Mental Routine: Combat (focus) Breath? Yes – No   Active Visualization? Yes - No   Passive Visualization? Yes - No

*Record your average times, and your best times. Constantly strive to push harder, while maintaining control. Note your best time. On smaller drills record averages and best times, but recording every repetition is not necessary.
**Maintain a speed where you can hit 90% accuracy in the combat effective zone with NO misses. Note where you lost control.

Drill 1: 1 shot X-Drill — Best Time

Times										
Key Notes:										

Drill 2: 2 shot X-Drill — Best Time

Times										
Key Notes:										

Drill 3: Acceleration/Deceleration Drill — Best Time

Times										
Key Notes:										

Drill 4: Multi-Hardcover Drill — Best Time

Key Notes:										
Key Notes:										

Copyright 2013, All rights reserved   www.shooting-performance.com

Competition Handgun Training Logbook

Drill 5 (extra work, shooters choice):										Best Time
Key Notes:										
Key Notes:										

Success Analysis: (What I did really well)

_____
_____
_____
_____

Solution Analysis: (What I figured out or need to figure out)

_____
_____
_____
_____

General Notes: (Any additional notes on the training session)

_____
_____
_____
_____

Carry Over (write any **key notes** you want to stand out to you in your next training session on that future log page):

_____
_____
_____
_____

Competition Handgun Training Logbook

General Details

** DID YOU REVIEW YOUR LAST TRAINING LOG FOR KEY INFORMATION BEFORE BEGINNING?? **

Training Phase: **2 Session B**   Date: _____   Weather: Sunny Cloudy Rain Snow Windy Temp: _____

Gun: _____   Problems? Yes - No   Ammo: _____   Problems? Yes - No

Mental Routine: Combat (focus) Breath? Yes – No   Active Visualization? Yes - No   Passive Visualization? Yes - No

*Record your average times, and your best times. Constantly strive to push harder, while maintaining control. Note your best time. On smaller drills record averages and best times, but recording every repetition is not necessary.
**Maintain a speed where you can hit 90% accuracy in the combat effective zone with NO misses. Note where you lost control.

Drill 1: Short Movement into Position | Best Time

Times											

Key Notes:

Drill 2: Long Movement into Position | Best Time

Times											

Key Notes:

Drill 3: Shooting and Moving Multi-Directional | Best Time

Times											

Key Notes:

Copyright 2013, All rights reserved   www.shooting-performance.com

Competition Handgun Training Logbook

Drill 4 (extra work, shooters choice):										Best Time
Key Notes:										
Key Notes:										

Success Analysis: (What I did really well)
_____
_____
_____
_____

Solution Analysis: (What I figured out or need to figure out)
_____
_____
_____
_____

General Notes: (Any additional notes on the training session)
_____
_____
_____
_____

Carry Over (write any **key notes** you want to stand out to you in your next training session on that future log page):
_____
_____
_____
_____

Competition Handgun Training Logbook

General Details

** DID YOU REVIEW YOUR LAST TRAINING LOG FOR KEY INFORMATION BEFORE BEGINNING?? **

Training Phase: **2 Session C**   Date: _____   Weather: Sunny Cloudy Rain Snow Windy Temp: _____

Gun: _____ Problems? Yes - No   Ammo: _____ Problems? Yes - No

Mental Routine: Combat (focus) Breath? Yes – No   Active Visualization? Yes - No   Passive Visualization? Yes - No

*Record your average times, and your best times. Constantly strive to push harder, while maintaining control. Note your best time. On smaller drills record averages and best times, but recording every repetition is not necessary.
**Maintain a speed where you can hit 90% accuracy in the combat effective zone with NO misses. Note where you lost control.

Drill 1: Multi-Position Drill — Best Time

Times										

Key Notes:

Drill 2: Strong and Weak Hand X-Drill — Best Time

Times										

Key Notes:

Drill 3: Long Range Challenge II — Best Time

Times										

Key Notes:

Competition Handgun Training Logbook

Drill 4: Off Balance Shooting											Best Time
Key Notes:											
Key Notes:											

Success Analysis: (What I did really well)

_____
_____
_____
_____

Solution Analysis: (What I figured out or need to figure out)

_____
_____
_____
_____

General Notes: (Any additional notes on the training session)

_____
_____
_____
_____

Carry Over (write any **key notes** you want to stand out to you in your next training session on that future log page):

_____
_____
_____
_____

Competition Handgun Training Logbook

General Details

** DID YOU REVIEW YOUR LAST TRAINING LOG FOR KEY INFORMATION BEFORE BEGINNING?? **

Training Phase: **2 Session A**   Date: _____   Weather: Sunny   Cloudy   Rain   Snow   Windy   Temp: _____

Gun: _____ Problems? Yes - No   Ammo: _____ Problems? Yes - No

Mental Routine: Combat (focus) Breath? Yes – No   Active Visualization? Yes - No   Passive Visualization? Yes - No

---

*Record your average times, and your best times. Constantly strive to push harder, while maintaining control. Note your best time. On smaller drills record averages and best times, but recording every repetition is not necessary.
**Maintain a speed where you can hit 90% accuracy in the combat effective zone with NO misses. Note where you lost control.

Drill 1: 1 shot X-Drill — Best Time

Times											
Key Notes:											

Drill 2: 2 shot X-Drill — Best Time

Times											
Key Notes:											

Drill 3: Acceleration/Deceleration Drill — Best Time

Times											
Key Notes:											

Drill 4: Multi-Hardcover Drill — Best Time

Key Notes:											
Key Notes:											

Copyright 2013, All rights reserved   www.shooting-performance.com

Competition Handgun Training Logbook

Drill 5 (extra work, shooters choice):										Best Time
Key Notes:										

Key Notes:

Success Analysis: (What I did really well)

_____
_____
_____
_____

Solution Analysis: (What I figured out or need to figure out)

_____
_____
_____
_____

General Notes: (Any additional notes on the training session)

_____
_____
_____
_____

Carry Over (write any **key notes** you want to stand out to you in your next training session on that future log page):

_____
_____
_____
_____

Competition Handgun Training Logbook

General Details

** DID YOU REVIEW YOUR LAST TRAINING LOG FOR KEY INFORMATION BEFORE BEGINNING?? **

Training Phase: **2 Session B**   Date: _____   Weather: Sunny Cloudy Rain Snow Windy Temp: _____

Gun: _____ Problems? Yes - No   Ammo: _____ Problems? Yes - No

Mental Routine: Combat (focus) Breath? Yes – No   Active Visualization? Yes - No   Passive Visualization? Yes - No

---

*Record your average times, and your best times. Constantly strive to push harder, while maintaining control. Note your best time. On smaller drills record averages and best times, but recording every repetition is not necessary.
**Maintain a speed where you can hit 90% accuracy in the combat effective zone with NO misses. Note where you lost control.

Drill 1: Short Movement into Position											Best Time
Times											
Key Notes:											

Drill 2: Long Movement into Position											Best Time
Times											
Key Notes:											

Drill 3: Shooting and Moving Multi-Directional											Best Time
Times											
Key Notes:											

Competition Handgun Training Logbook

Drill 4 (extra work, shooters choice):											Best Time
Key Notes:											
Key Notes:											

Success Analysis: (What I did really well)

_____
_____
_____
_____

Solution Analysis: (What I figured out or need to figure out)

_____
_____
_____
_____

General Notes: (Any additional notes on the training session)

_____
_____
_____
_____

Carry Over (write any **key notes** you want to stand out to you in your next training session on that future log page):

_____
_____
_____
_____

Competition Handgun Training Logbook

General Details

** DID YOU REVIEW YOUR LAST TRAINING LOG FOR KEY INFORMATION BEFORE BEGINNING?? **

Training Phase: **2 Session C**   Date: _____   Weather: Sunny   Cloudy   Rain   Snow   Windy   Temp: _____

Gun: _____ Problems? Yes - No   Ammo: _____ Problems? Yes - No

Mental Routine: Combat (focus) Breath? Yes – No   Active Visualization? Yes - No   Passive Visualization? Yes - No

---

*Record your average times, and your best times. Constantly strive to push harder, while maintaining control. Note your best time. On smaller drills record averages and best times, but recording every repetition is not necessary.
**Maintain a speed where you can hit 90% accuracy in the combat effective zone with NO misses. Note where you lost control.

Drill 1: Multi-Position Drill | Best Time

Times										

Key Notes:

Drill 2: Strong and Weak Hand X-Drill | Best Time

Times										

Key Notes:

Drill 3: Long Range Challenge II | Best Time

Times										

Key Notes:

Competition Handgun Training Logbook

Drill 4: Off Balance Shooting										Best Time
Key Notes:										
Key Notes:										

Success Analysis: (What I did really well)

_____
_____
_____
_____

Solution Analysis: (What I figured out or need to figure out)

_____
_____
_____
_____

General Notes: (Any additional notes on the training session)

_____
_____
_____
_____

Carry Over (write any **key notes** you want to stand out to you in your next training session on that future log page):

_____
_____
_____
_____

Competition Handgun Training Logbook

General Details

** DID YOU REVIEW YOUR LAST TRAINING LOG FOR KEY INFORMATION BEFORE BEGINNING?? **

Training Phase: **2 Session A**   Date: _____   Weather: Sunny Cloudy Rain Snow Windy   Temp: _____

Gun: _____ Problems? Yes - No   Ammo: _____ Problems? Yes - No

Mental Routine: Combat (focus) Breath? Yes – No   Active Visualization? Yes - No   Passive Visualization? Yes - No

---

*Record your average times, and your best times. Constantly strive to push harder, while maintaining control. Note your best time. On smaller drills record averages and best times, but recording every repetition is not necessary.
**Maintain a speed where you can hit 90% accuracy in the combat effective zone with NO misses. Note where you lost control.

Drill 1: 1 shot X-Drill — Best Time

Times											

Key Notes:

Drill 2: 2 shot X-Drill — Best Time

Times											

Key Notes:

Drill 3: Acceleration/Deceleration Drill — Best Time

Times											

Key Notes:

Drill 4: Multi-Hardcover Drill — Best Time

Key Notes:											

Key Notes:

Competition Handgun Training Logbook

Drill 5 (extra work, shooters choice):										Best Time
Key Notes:										
Key Notes:										

Success Analysis: (What I did really well)

_____
_____
_____
_____

Solution Analysis: (What I figured out or need to figure out)

_____
_____
_____
_____

General Notes: (Any additional notes on the training session)

_____
_____
_____
_____
_____

Carry Over (write any **key notes** you want to stand out to you in your next training session on that future log page):

_____
_____
_____
_____

Competition Handgun Training Logbook

General Details

** DID YOU REVIEW YOUR LAST TRAINING LOG FOR KEY INFORMATION BEFORE BEGINNING?? **

Training Phase: **2 Session B**   Date: _____   Weather: Sunny Cloudy Rain Snow Windy Temp: _____

Gun: _____ Problems? Yes - No   Ammo: _____ Problems? Yes - No

Mental Routine: Combat (focus) Breath? Yes – No   Active Visualization? Yes - No   Passive Visualization? Yes - No

*Record your average times, and your best times. Constantly strive to push harder, while maintaining control. Note your best time. On smaller drills record averages and best times, but recording every repetition is not necessary.
**Maintain a speed where you can hit 90% accuracy in the combat effective zone with NO misses. Note where you lost control.

Drill 1: Short Movement into Position										Best Time
Times										
Key Notes:										

Drill 2: Long Movement into Position										Best Time
Times										
Key Notes:										

Drill 3: Shooting and Moving Multi-Directional										Best Time
Times										
Key Notes:										

Competition Handgun Training Logbook

Drill 4 (extra work, shooters choice):										Best Time
Key Notes:										
Key Notes:										

Success Analysis: (What I did really well)

_____
_____
_____
_____

Solution Analysis: (What I figured out or need to figure out)

_____
_____
_____
_____

General Notes: (Any additional notes on the training session)

_____
_____
_____
_____

Carry Over (write any **key notes** you want to stand out to you in your next training session on that future log page):

_____
_____
_____
_____

Competition Handgun Training Logbook

General Details

** DID YOU REVIEW YOUR LAST TRAINING LOG FOR KEY INFORMATION BEFORE BEGINNING?? **

Training Phase: **2 Session C**   Date: _____   Weather: Sunny Cloudy Rain Snow Windy Temp: _____

Gun: _____   Problems? Yes - No   Ammo: _____   Problems? Yes - No

Mental Routine: Combat (focus) Breath? Yes – No   Active Visualization? Yes - No   Passive Visualization? Yes - No

---

*Record your average times, and your best times. Constantly strive to push harder, while maintaining control. Note your best time. On smaller drills record averages and best times, but recording every repetition is not necessary.
**Maintain a speed where you can hit 90% accuracy in the combat effective zone with NO misses. Note where you lost control.

Drill 1: Multi-Position Drill											Best Time
Times											
Key Notes:											

Drill 2: Strong and Weak Hand X-Drill											Best Time
Times											
Key Notes:											

Drill 3: Long Range Challenge II											Best Time
Times											
Key Notes:											

Competition Handgun Training Logbook

Drill 4: Off Balance Shooting											Best Time
Key Notes:											
Key Notes:											

Success Analysis: (What I did really well)
_____
_____
_____
_____

Solution Analysis: (What I figured out or need to figure out)
_____
_____
_____
_____

General Notes: (Any additional notes on the training session)
_____
_____
_____
_____

Carry Over (write any **key notes** you want to stand out to you in your next training session on that future log page):
_____
_____
_____
_____

You have completed **Phase Two**! Accomplish the following before beginning Phase Three:

- Assess whether you are ready to begin Phase Three. If necessary, you may repeat some of the Phase Two training sessions before continuing on.
- Rest and review. This is your chance to rest and take a week off from training. Review your Phase Two notes and prepare yourself physically and mentally to begin the next session.

Phase Two Notes:

_____
_____
_____
_____
_____
_____
_____
_____
_____
_____
_____
_____
_____
_____
_____
_____

Begin Phase Three

Competition Handgun Training Logbook

General Details

** DID YOU REVIEW YOUR LAST TRAINING LOG FOR KEY INFORMATION BEFORE BEGINNING?? **

Training Phase: **3 Session A**   Date: _____   Weather: Sunny Cloudy Rain Snow Windy Temp: _____

Gun: _____ Problems? Yes - No   Ammo: _____ Problems? Yes - No

Mental Routine: Combat (focus) Breath? Yes – No   Active Visualization? Yes - No   Passive Visualization? Yes - No

*Record your average times, and your best times. Constantly strive to push harder, while maintaining control. Note your best time. On smaller drills record averages and best times, but recording every repetition is not necessary.
**Maintain a speed where you can hit 90% accuracy in the combat effective zone with NO misses. Note where you lost control.

Drill 1: 1 shot X-Drill (phase 3)   Best Time

Times										

Key Notes:

Drill 2: 2 shot X-Drill (phase 3)   Best Time

Times										

Key Notes:

Drill 3: Barricade X-Drill   Best Time

Times										

Key Notes:

Drill 4: Multiple Distance with Reload   Best Time

Key Notes:										

Key Notes:

Copyright 2013, All rights reserved   www.shooting-performance.com

Competition Handgun Training Logbook

Drill 5 (extra work, shooters choice):									Best Time
Key Notes:									
Key Notes:									

Success Analysis: (What I did really well)

_____
_____
_____
_____

Solution Analysis: (What I figured out or need to figure out)

_____
_____
_____
_____

General Notes: (Any additional notes on the training session)

_____
_____
_____
_____

Carry Over (write any **key notes** you want to stand out to you in your next training session on that future log page):

_____
_____
_____
_____

Competition Handgun Training Logbook

General Details

** DID YOU REVIEW YOUR LAST TRAINING LOG FOR KEY INFORMATION BEFORE BEGINNING?? **

Training Phase: **3 Session B**   Date: _____   Weather: Sunny Cloudy Rain Snow Windy Temp: _____

Gun: _____ Problems? Yes - No   Ammo: _____ Problems? Yes - No

Mental Routine: Combat (focus) Breath? Yes – No   Active Visualization? Yes - No   Passive Visualization? Yes - No

---

*Record your average times, and your best times. Constantly strive to push harder, while maintaining control. Note your best time. On smaller drills record averages and best times, but recording every repetition is not necessary.
**Maintain a speed where you can hit 90% accuracy in the combat effective zone with NO misses. Note where you lost control.

Drill 1: Shooting and Moving, Aggressive Entry										Best Time
Times										
Key Notes:										

Drill 2: Shooting and Moving, Multidirectional										Best Time
Times										
Key Notes:										

Drill 3: Moving Reload										Best Time
Times										
Key Notes:										

Copyright 2013, All rights reserved   www.shooting-performance.com

Competition Handgun Training Logbook

Drill 4 (extra work, shooters choice):											Best Time
Key Notes:											
Key Notes:											

Success Analysis: (What I did really well)

_____
_____
_____
_____

Solution Analysis: (What I figured out or need to figure out)

_____
_____
_____
_____

General Notes: (Any additional notes on the training session)

_____
_____
_____
_____

Carry Over (write any **key notes** you want to stand out to you in your next training session on that future log page):

_____
_____
_____
_____

Competition Handgun Training Logbook

General Details

** DID YOU REVIEW YOUR LAST TRAINING LOG FOR KEY INFORMATION BEFORE BEGINNING?? **

Training Phase: **3 Session C**   Date: _____   Weather: Sunny Cloudy Rain Snow Windy Temp: _____

Gun: _____ Problems? Yes - No   Ammo: _____ Problems? Yes - No

Mental Routine: Combat (focus) Breath? Yes – No   Active Visualization? Yes - No   Passive Visualization? Yes - No

*Record your average times, and your best times. Constantly strive to push harder, while maintaining control. Note your best time. On smaller drills record averages and best times, but recording every repetition is not necessary.
**Maintain a speed where you can hit 90% accuracy in the combat effective zone with NO misses. Note where you lost control.

Drill 1: Strong and Weak Hand X-Drill (phase 3) — Best Time

Times											

Key Notes:

Drill 2: Multi-Port Drill — Best Time

Times											

Key Notes:

Drill 3: Long Range Challenge III — Best Time

Times											

Key Notes:

Competition Handgun Training Logbook

Drill 4: Target Acquisition										Best Time
Key Notes:										
Key Notes:										

Success Analysis: (What I did really well)

_____
_____
_____
_____

Solution Analysis: (What I figured out or need to figure out)

_____
_____
_____
_____

General Notes: (Any additional notes on the training session)

_____
_____
_____
_____

Carry Over (write any **key notes** you want to stand out to you in your next training session on that future log page):

_____
_____
_____
_____

Competition Handgun Training Logbook

General Details

** DID YOU REVIEW YOUR LAST TRAINING LOG FOR KEY INFORMATION BEFORE BEGINNING?? **

Training Phase: **3 Session A**   Date: _____   Weather: Sunny Cloudy Rain Snow Windy Temp: _____

Gun: _____ Problems? Yes - No   Ammo: _____ Problems? Yes - No

Mental Routine: Combat (focus) Breath? Yes – No   Active Visualization? Yes - No   Passive Visualization? Yes - No

*Record your average times, and your best times. Constantly strive to push harder, while maintaining control. Note your best time. On smaller drills record averages and best times, but recording every repetition is not necessary.
**Maintain a speed where you can hit 90% accuracy in the combat effective zone with NO misses. Note where you lost control.

Drill 1: 1 shot X-Drill (phase 3)											Best Time
Times											
Key Notes:											

Drill 2: 2 shot X-Drill (phase 3)											Best Time
Times											
Key Notes:											

Drill 3: Barricade X-Drill											Best Time
Times											
Key Notes:											

Drill 4: Multiple Distance with Reload											Best Time
Key Notes:											
Key Notes:											

Copyright 2013, All rights reserved   www.shooting-performance.com

Competition Handgun Training Logbook

Drill 5 (extra work, shooters choice):										Best Time
Key Notes:										
Key Notes:										

Success Analysis: (What I did really well)

_____
_____
_____
_____

Solution Analysis: (What I figured out or need to figure out)

_____
_____
_____
_____

General Notes: (Any additional notes on the training session)

_____
_____
_____
_____

Carry Over (write any **key notes** you want to stand out to you in your next training session on that future log page):

_____
_____
_____
_____

Competition Handgun Training Logbook

General Details

** DID YOU REVIEW YOUR LAST TRAINING LOG FOR KEY INFORMATION BEFORE BEGINNING?? **

Training Phase: **3 Session B**   Date: _____   Weather: Sunny Cloudy Rain Snow Windy Temp: _____

Gun: _____ Problems? Yes - No   Ammo: _____ Problems? Yes - No

Mental Routine: Combat (focus) Breath? Yes – No   Active Visualization? Yes - No   Passive Visualization? Yes - No

*Record your average times, and your best times. Constantly strive to push harder, while maintaining control. Note your best time. On smaller drills record averages and best times, but recording every repetition is not necessary.
**Maintain a speed where you can hit 90% accuracy in the combat effective zone with NO misses. Note where you lost control.

Drill 1: Shooting and Moving, Aggressive Entry — Best Time

Times										

Key Notes:

Drill 2: Shooting and Moving, Multidirectional — Best Time

Times										

Key Notes:

Drill 3: Moving Reload — Best Time

Times										

Key Notes:

Competition Handgun Training Logbook

Drill 4 (extra work, shooters choice):										Best Time
Key Notes:										
Key Notes:										

Success Analysis: (What I did really well)

_____
_____
_____
_____

Solution Analysis: (What I figured out or need to figure out)

_____
_____
_____
_____

General Notes: (Any additional notes on the training session)

_____
_____
_____
_____

Carry Over (write any **key notes** you want to stand out to you in your next training session on that future log page):

_____
_____
_____
_____

Competition Handgun Training Logbook

General Details

** DID YOU REVIEW YOUR LAST TRAINING LOG FOR KEY INFORMATION BEFORE BEGINNING?? **

Training Phase: **3 Session C**   Date: _____   Weather: Sunny Cloudy Rain Snow Windy Temp: _____

Gun: _____ Problems? Yes - No   Ammo: _____ Problems? Yes - No

Mental Routine: Combat (focus) Breath? Yes – No   Active Visualization? Yes - No   Passive Visualization? Yes - No

*Record your average times, and your best times. Constantly strive to push harder, while maintaining control. Note your best time. On smaller drills record averages and best times, but recording every repetition is not necessary.
**Maintain a speed where you can hit 90% accuracy in the combat effective zone with NO misses. Note where you lost control.

Drill 1: Strong and Weak Hand X-Drill (phase 3) — Best Time

Times										

Key Notes:

Drill 2: Multi-Port Drill — Best Time

Times										

Key Notes:

Drill 3: Long Range Challenge III — Best Time

Times										

Key Notes:

Competition Handgun Training Logbook

Drill 4: Target Acquisition											Best Time
Key Notes:											
Key Notes:											

Success Analysis: (What I did really well)

_____
_____
_____
_____

Solution Analysis: (What I figured out or need to figure out)

_____
_____
_____
_____

General Notes: (Any additional notes on the training session)

_____
_____
_____
_____

Carry Over (write any **key notes** you want to stand out to you in your next training session on that future log page):

_____
_____
_____
_____

Competition Handgun Training Logbook

General Details

** DID YOU REVIEW YOUR LAST TRAINING LOG FOR KEY INFORMATION BEFORE BEGINNING?? **

Training Phase: **3 Session A**   Date: _____   Weather: Sunny   Cloudy   Rain   Snow   Windy   Temp: _____

Gun: _____   Problems? Yes - No   Ammo: _____   Problems? Yes - No

Mental Routine: Combat (focus) Breath? Yes – No   Active Visualization? Yes - No   Passive Visualization? Yes - No

*Record your average times, and your best times. Constantly strive to push harder, while maintaining control. Note your best time. On smaller drills record averages and best times, but recording every repetition is not necessary.
**Maintain a speed where you can hit 90% accuracy in the combat effective zone with NO misses. Note where you lost control.

Drill 1: 1 shot X-Drill (phase 3)   Best Time

Times											
Key Notes:											

Drill 2: 2 shot X-Drill (phase 3)   Best Time

Times											
Key Notes:											

Drill 3: Barricade X-Drill   Best Time

Times											
Key Notes:											

Drill 4: Multiple Distance with Reload   Best Time

Key Notes:											
Key Notes:											

Competition Handgun Training Logbook

Drill 5 (extra work, shooters choice):										Best Time
Key Notes:										
Key Notes:										

Success Analysis: (What I did really well)

_____
_____
_____
_____

Solution Analysis: (What I figured out or need to figure out)

_____
_____
_____
_____

General Notes: (Any additional notes on the training session)

_____
_____
_____
_____

Carry Over (write any **key notes** you want to stand out to you in your next training session on that future log page):

_____
_____
_____
_____

Copyright 2013, All rights reserved   www.shooting-performance.com

Competition Handgun Training Logbook

General Details

** DID YOU REVIEW YOUR LAST TRAINING LOG FOR KEY INFORMATION BEFORE BEGINNING?? **

Training Phase: **3 Session B**   Date: _____   Weather: Sunny Cloudy Rain Snow Windy   Temp: _____

Gun: _____ Problems? Yes - No   Ammo: _____ Problems? Yes - No

Mental Routine: Combat (focus) Breath? Yes – No   Active Visualization? Yes - No   Passive Visualization? Yes - No

---

*Record your average times, and your best times. Constantly strive to push harder, while maintaining control. Note your best time. On smaller drills record averages and best times, but recording every repetition is not necessary.
**Maintain a speed where you can hit 90% accuracy in the combat effective zone with NO misses. Note where you lost control.

Drill 1: Shooting and Moving, Aggressive Entry — Best Time

Times										

Key Notes:

Drill 2: Shooting and Moving, Multidirectional — Best Time

Times										

Key Notes:

Drill 3: Moving Reload — Best Time

Times										

Key Notes:

Competition Handgun Training Logbook

Drill 4 (extra work, shooters choice):										Best Time
Key Notes:										
Key Notes:										

Success Analysis: (What I did really well)

_____
_____
_____
_____

Solution Analysis: (What I figured out or need to figure out)

_____
_____
_____
_____

General Notes: (Any additional notes on the training session)

_____
_____
_____
_____

Carry Over (write any **key notes** you want to stand out to you in your next training session on that future log page):

_____
_____
_____
_____

Competition Handgun Training Logbook

General Details

** DID YOU REVIEW YOUR LAST TRAINING LOG FOR KEY INFORMATION BEFORE BEGINNING?? **

Training Phase: **3 Session C** Date: _____ Weather: Sunny Cloudy Rain Snow Windy Temp: _____

Gun: _____ Problems? Yes - No Ammo: _____ Problems? Yes - No

Mental Routine: Combat (focus) Breath? Yes – No   Active Visualization? Yes - No   Passive Visualization? Yes - No

---

*Record your average times, and your best times. Constantly strive to push harder, while maintaining control. Note your best time. On smaller drills record averages and best times, but recording every repetition is not necessary.
**Maintain a speed where you can hit 90% accuracy in the combat effective zone with NO misses. Note where you lost control.

Drill 1: Strong and Weak Hand X-Drill (phase 3)										Best Time
Times										
Key Notes:										

Drill 2: Multi-Port Drill										Best Time
Times										
Key Notes:										

Drill 3: Long Range Challenge III										Best Time
Times										
Key Notes:										

Copyright 2013, All rights reserved   www.shooting-performance.com

Competition Handgun Training Logbook

Drill 4: Target Acquisition										Best Time
Key Notes:										
Key Notes:										

Success Analysis: (What I did really well)

_____
_____
_____
_____

Solution Analysis: (What I figured out or need to figure out)

_____
_____
_____
_____

General Notes: (Any additional notes on the training session)

_____
_____
_____
_____

Carry Over (write any **key notes** you want to stand out to you in your next training session on that future log page):

_____
_____
_____
_____

Competition Handgun Training Logbook

General Details

** DID YOU REVIEW YOUR LAST TRAINING LOG FOR KEY INFORMATION BEFORE BEGINNING?? **

Training Phase: **3 Session A**   Date: _____   Weather: Sunny Cloudy Rain Snow Windy   Temp: _____

Gun: _____ Problems? Yes - No   Ammo: _____ Problems? Yes - No

Mental Routine: Combat (focus) Breath? Yes – No   Active Visualization? Yes - No   Passive Visualization? Yes - No

*Record your average times, and your best times. Constantly strive to push harder, while maintaining control. Note your best time. On smaller drills record averages and best times, but recording every repetition is not necessary.
**Maintain a speed where you can hit 90% accuracy in the combat effective zone with NO misses. Note where you lost control.

Drill 1: 1 shot X-Drill (phase 3) — Best Time

Times										

Key Notes:

Drill 2: 2 shot X-Drill (phase 3) — Best Time

Times										

Key Notes:

Drill 3: Barricade X-Drill — Best Time

Times										

Key Notes:

Drill 4: Multiple Distance with Reload — Best Time

Key Notes:										

Key Notes:

Copyright 2013, All rights reserved   www.shooting-performance.com

Competition Handgun Training Logbook

Drill 5 (extra work, shooters choice):										Best Time
Key Notes:										
Key Notes:										

Success Analysis: (What I did really well)
_____
_____
_____
_____

Solution Analysis: (What I figured out or need to figure out)
_____
_____
_____
_____

General Notes: (Any additional notes on the training session)
_____
_____
_____
_____

Carry Over (write any **key notes** you want to stand out to you in your next training session on that future log page):
_____
_____
_____
_____

Competition Handgun Training Logbook

General Details

** DID YOU REVIEW YOUR LAST TRAINING LOG FOR KEY INFORMATION BEFORE BEGINNING?? **

Training Phase: **3 Session B**   Date: _____   Weather: Sunny Cloudy Rain Snow Windy Temp: _____

Gun: _____ Problems? Yes - No   Ammo: _____ Problems? Yes - No

Mental Routine: Combat (focus) Breath? Yes – No   Active Visualization? Yes - No   Passive Visualization? Yes - No

*Record your average times, and your best times. Constantly strive to push harder, while maintaining control. Note your best time. On smaller drills record averages and best times, but recording every repetition is not necessary.
**Maintain a speed where you can hit 90% accuracy in the combat effective zone with NO misses. Note where you lost control.

Drill 1: Shooting and Moving, Aggressive Entry — Best Time

Times										

Key Notes:

Drill 2: Shooting and Moving, Multidirectional — Best Time

Times										

Key Notes:

Drill 3: Moving Reload — Best Time

Times										

Key Notes:

Drill 4 (extra work, shooters choice):											Best Time
Key Notes:											
Key Notes:											

Success Analysis: (What I did really well)

_____
_____
_____
_____

Solution Analysis: (What I figured out or need to figure out)

_____
_____
_____
_____

General Notes: (Any additional notes on the training session)

_____
_____
_____
_____

Carry Over (write any **key notes** you want to stand out to you in your next training session on that future log page):

_____
_____
_____
_____

Competition Handgun Training Logbook

General Details

** DID YOU REVIEW YOUR LAST TRAINING LOG FOR KEY INFORMATION BEFORE BEGINNING?? **

Training Phase: **3 Session C**   Date: _____   Weather: Sunny Cloudy Rain Snow Windy Temp: _____

Gun: _____ Problems? Yes - No   Ammo: _____ Problems? Yes - No

Mental Routine: Combat (focus) Breath? Yes – No   Active Visualization? Yes - No   Passive Visualization? Yes - No

*Record your average times, and your best times. Constantly strive to push harder, while maintaining control. Note your best time. On smaller drills record averages and best times, but recording every repetition is not necessary.
**Maintain a speed where you can hit 90% accuracy in the combat effective zone with NO misses. Note where you lost control.

Drill 1: Strong and Weak Hand X-Drill (phase 3) — Best Time

Times										

Key Notes:

Drill 2: Multi-Port Drill — Best Time

Times										

Key Notes:

Drill 3: Long Range Challenge III — Best Time

Times										

Key Notes:

Copyright 2013, All rights reserved   www.shooting-performance.com

Competition Handgun Training Logbook

Drill 4: Target Acquisition										Best Time
Key Notes:										
Key Notes:										

Success Analysis: (What I did really well)

_____
_____
_____
_____

Solution Analysis: (What I figured out or need to figure out)

_____
_____
_____
_____

General Notes: (Any additional notes on the training session)

_____
_____
_____
_____

Carry Over (write any **key notes** you want to stand out to you in your next training session on that future log page):

_____
_____
_____
_____

Competition Handgun Training Logbook

General Details

** DID YOU REVIEW YOUR LAST TRAINING LOG FOR KEY INFORMATION BEFORE BEGINNING?? **

Training Phase: **3 Session A**   Date: _____   Weather: Sunny Cloudy Rain Snow Windy   Temp: _____

Gun: _____ Problems? Yes - No   Ammo: _____ Problems? Yes - No

Mental Routine: Combat (focus) Breath? Yes – No   Active Visualization? Yes - No   Passive Visualization? Yes - No

*Record your average times, and your best times. Constantly strive to push harder, while maintaining control. Note your best time. On smaller drills record averages and best times, but recording every repetition is not necessary.
**Maintain a speed where you can hit 90% accuracy in the combat effective zone with NO misses. Note where you lost control.

Drill 1: 1 shot X-Drill (phase 3) — Best Time

Times										
Key Notes:										

Drill 2: 2 shot X-Drill (phase 3) — Best Time

Times										
Key Notes:										

Drill 3: Barricade X-Drill — Best Time

Times										
Key Notes:										

Drill 4: Multiple Distance with Reload — Best Time

Key Notes:										
Key Notes:										

Competition Handgun Training Logbook

Drill 5 (extra work, shooters choice):										Best Time
Key Notes:										
Key Notes:										

Success Analysis: (What I did really well)
_____
_____
_____
_____
_____

Solution Analysis: (What I figured out or need to figure out)
_____
_____
_____
_____
_____

General Notes: (Any additional notes on the training session)
_____
_____
_____
_____
_____

Carry Over (write any **key notes** you want to stand out to you in your next training session on that future log page):
_____
_____
_____
_____

Competition Handgun Training Logbook

General Details

** DID YOU REVIEW YOUR LAST TRAINING LOG FOR KEY INFORMATION BEFORE BEGINNING?? **

Training Phase: **3 Session B**   Date: _____   Weather: Sunny Cloudy Rain Snow Windy Temp: _____

Gun: _____ Problems? Yes - No   Ammo: _____ Problems? Yes - No

Mental Routine: Combat (focus) Breath? Yes – No   Active Visualization? Yes - No   Passive Visualization? Yes - No

*Record your average times, and your best times. Constantly strive to push harder, while maintaining control. Note your best time. On smaller drills record averages and best times, but recording every repetition is not necessary.
**Maintain a speed where you can hit 90% accuracy in the combat effective zone with NO misses. Note where you lost control.

Drill 1: Shooting and Moving, Aggressive Entry										Best Time
Times										
Key Notes:										

Drill 2: Shooting and Moving, Multidirectional										Best Time
Times										
Key Notes:										

Drill 3: Moving Reload										Best Time
Times										
Key Notes:										

Copyright 2013, All rights reserved   www.shooting-performance.com

Competition Handgun Training Logbook

Drill 4 (extra work, shooters choice):										Best Time
Key Notes:										
Key Notes:										

Success Analysis: (What I did really well)

_____
_____
_____
_____

Solution Analysis: (What I figured out or need to figure out)

_____
_____
_____
_____

General Notes: (Any additional notes on the training session)

_____
_____
_____
_____

Carry Over (write any **key notes** you want to stand out to you in your next training session on that future log page):

_____
_____
_____
_____

Competition Handgun Training Logbook

General Details

** DID YOU REVIEW YOUR LAST TRAINING LOG FOR KEY INFORMATION BEFORE BEGINNING?? **

Training Phase: **3 Session C**   Date: _____   Weather: Sunny Cloudy Rain Snow Windy   Temp: _____

Gun: _____   Problems? Yes - No   Ammo: _____   Problems? Yes - No

Mental Routine: Combat (focus) Breath? Yes – No   Active Visualization? Yes - No   Passive Visualization? Yes - No

*Record your average times, and your best times. Constantly strive to push harder, while maintaining control. Note your best time. On smaller drills record averages and best times, but recording every repetition is not necessary.
**Maintain a speed where you can hit 90% accuracy in the combat effective zone with NO misses. Note where you lost control.

Drill 1: Strong and Weak Hand X-Drill (phase 3) — Best Time

Times										

Key Notes:

Drill 2: Multi-Port Drill — Best Time

Times										

Key Notes:

Drill 3: Long Range Challenge III — Best Time

Times										

Key Notes:

Competition Handgun Training Logbook

Drill 4: Target Acquisition										Best Time
Key Notes:										
Key Notes:										

Success Analysis: (What I did really well)

_____
_____
_____
_____

Solution Analysis: (What I figured out or need to figure out)

_____
_____
_____
_____

General Notes: (Any additional notes on the training session)

_____
_____
_____
_____

Carry Over (write any **key notes** you want to stand out to you in your next training session on that future log page):

_____
_____
_____
_____

Competition Handgun Training Logbook

General Details

** DID YOU REVIEW YOUR LAST TRAINING LOG FOR KEY INFORMATION BEFORE BEGINNING?? **

Training Phase: **3 Session A**   Date: _____   Weather: Sunny Cloudy Rain Snow Windy   Temp: _____

Gun: _____ Problems? Yes - No   Ammo: _____ Problems? Yes - No

Mental Routine: Combat (focus) Breath? Yes – No   Active Visualization? Yes - No   Passive Visualization? Yes - No

*Record your average times, and your best times. Constantly strive to push harder, while maintaining control. Note your best time. On smaller drills record averages and best times, but recording every repetition is not necessary.
**Maintain a speed where you can hit 90% accuracy in the combat effective zone with NO misses. Note where you lost control.

Drill 1: 1 shot X-Drill (phase 3) — Best Time

Times										

Key Notes:

Drill 2: 2 shot X-Drill (phase 3) — Best Time

Times										

Key Notes:

Drill 3: Barricade X-Drill — Best Time

Times										

Key Notes:

Drill 4: Multiple Distance with Reload — Best Time

Key Notes:										

Key Notes:

Competition Handgun Training Logbook

Drill 5 (extra work, shooters choice):											Best Time
Key Notes:											
Key Notes:											

Success Analysis: (What I did really well)

_____
_____
_____
_____

Solution Analysis: (What I figured out or need to figure out)

_____
_____
_____
_____

General Notes: (Any additional notes on the training session)

_____
_____
_____
_____

Carry Over (write any **key notes** you want to stand out to you in your next training session on that future log page):

_____
_____
_____
_____

Competition Handgun Training Logbook

General Details

** DID YOU REVIEW YOUR LAST TRAINING LOG FOR KEY INFORMATION BEFORE BEGINNING?? **

Training Phase: **3 Session B**   Date: _____   Weather: Sunny Cloudy Rain Snow Windy Temp: _____

Gun: _____ Problems? Yes - No   Ammo: _____ Problems? Yes - No

Mental Routine: Combat (focus) Breath? Yes – No   Active Visualization? Yes - No   Passive Visualization? Yes - No

*Record your average times, and your best times. Constantly strive to push harder, while maintaining control. Note your best time. On smaller drills record averages and best times, but recording every repetition is not necessary.
**Maintain a speed where you can hit 90% accuracy in the combat effective zone with NO misses. Note where you lost control.

Drill 1: Shooting and Moving, Aggressive Entry   Best Time

Times										
Key Notes:										

Drill 2: Shooting and Moving, Multidirectional   Best Time

Times										
Key Notes:										

Drill 3: Moving Reload   Best Time

Times										
Key Notes:										

Copyright 2013, All rights reserved   www.shooting-performance.com

Competition Handgun Training Logbook

Drill 4 (extra work, shooters choice):										Best Time
Key Notes:										
Key Notes:										

Success Analysis: (What I did really well)

_____
_____
_____
_____

Solution Analysis: (What I figured out or need to figure out)

_____
_____
_____
_____

General Notes: (Any additional notes on the training session)

_____
_____
_____
_____
_____

Carry Over (write any **key notes** you want to stand out to you in your next training session on that future log page):

_____
_____
_____
_____

Competition Handgun Training Logbook

General Details

** DID YOU REVIEW YOUR LAST TRAINING LOG FOR KEY INFORMATION BEFORE BEGINNING?? **

Training Phase: **3 Session C**   Date: _____   Weather: Sunny Cloudy Rain Snow Windy Temp: _____

Gun: _____ Problems? Yes - No Ammo: _____ Problems? Yes - No

Mental Routine: Combat (focus) Breath? Yes – No   Active Visualization? Yes - No   Passive Visualization? Yes - No

*Record your average times, and your best times. Constantly strive to push harder, while maintaining control. Note your best time. On smaller drills record averages and best times, but recording every repetition is not necessary.
**Maintain a speed where you can hit 90% accuracy in the combat effective zone with NO misses. Note where you lost control.

Drill 1: Strong and Weak Hand X-Drill (phase 3)	Best Time

Times										

Key Notes:

Drill 2: Multi-Port Drill	Best Time

Times										

Key Notes:

Drill 3: Long Range Challenge III	Best Time

Times										

Key Notes:

Competition Handgun Training Logbook

Drill 4: Target Acquisition											Best Time
Key Notes:											

Key Notes:

Success Analysis: (What I did really well)
___
___
___
___
___

Solution Analysis: (What I figured out or need to figure out)
___
___
___
___
___

General Notes: (Any additional notes on the training session)
___
___
___
___
___

Carry Over (write any **key notes** you want to stand out to you in your next training session on that future log page):
___
___
___
___

Competition Handgun Training Logbook

General Details

** DID YOU REVIEW YOUR LAST TRAINING LOG FOR KEY INFORMATION BEFORE BEGINNING?? **

Extra Session: _____ Date: _____ Weather: Sunny Cloudy Rain Snow Windy Temp: _____

Gun: _____ Problems? Yes - No   Ammo: _____ Problems? Yes - No

Mental Routine: Combat (focus) Breath? Yes – No   Active Visualization? Yes - No   Passive Visualization? Yes - No

---

*Record your average times, and your best times. Constantly strive to push harder, while maintaining control. Note your best time. On smaller drills record averages and best times, but recording every repetition is not necessary.

**Maintain a speed where you can hit 90% accuracy in the combat effective zone with NO misses. Note where you lost control.

Drill 1:										Best Time
Times									
Key Notes:									

Drill 2:										Best Time
Times									
Key Notes:									

Drill 3:										Best Time
Times									
Key Notes:									

Competition Handgun Training Logbook

Drill 4:										Best Time
Key Notes:										
Key Notes:										

Success Analysis: (What I did really well)
_____
_____
_____
_____

Solution Analysis: (What I figured out or need to figure out)
_____
_____
_____
_____

General Notes: (Any additional notes on the training session)
_____
_____
_____
_____

Carry Over (write any **key notes** you want to stand out to you in your next training session on that future log page):
_____
_____
_____
_____

Competition Handgun Training Logbook

General Details

** DID YOU REVIEW YOUR LAST TRAINING LOG FOR KEY INFORMATION BEFORE BEGINNING?? **

Extra Session: _____ Date: _____ Weather: Sunny Cloudy Rain Snow Windy Temp: _____

Gun: _____ Problems? Yes - No   Ammo: _____ Problems? Yes - No

Mental Routine: Combat (focus) Breath? Yes – No   Active Visualization? Yes - No   Passive Visualization? Yes - No

---

*Record your average times, and your best times. Constantly strive to push harder, while maintaining control. Note your best time. On smaller drills record averages and best times, but recording every repetition is not necessary.

**Maintain a speed where you can hit 90% accuracy in the combat effective zone with NO misses. Note where you lost control.

Drill 1: | Best Time

Times										

Key Notes:

Drill 2: | Best Time

Times										

Key Notes:

Drill 3: | Best Time

Times										

Key Notes:

Competition Handgun Training Logbook

Drill 4:											Best Time
Key Notes:											
Key Notes:											

Success Analysis: (What I did really well)
_____
_____
_____
_____

Solution Analysis: (What I figured out or need to figure out)
_____
_____
_____
_____

General Notes: (Any additional notes on the training session)
_____
_____
_____
_____

Carry Over (write any **key notes** you want to stand out to you in your next training session on that future log page):
_____
_____
_____
_____

Competition Handgun Training Logbook

General Details

** DID YOU REVIEW YOUR LAST TRAINING LOG FOR KEY INFORMATION BEFORE BEGINNING?? **

Extra Session: _____ Date: _____ Weather: Sunny Cloudy Rain Snow Windy Temp: _____

Gun: _____ Problems? Yes - No Ammo: _____ Problems? Yes - No

Mental Routine: Combat (focus) Breath? Yes – No Active Visualization? Yes - No   Passive Visualization? Yes - No

*Record your average times, and your best times. Constantly strive to push harder, while maintaining control. Note your best time. On smaller drills record averages and best times, but recording every repetition is not necessary.
**Maintain a speed where you can hit 90% accuracy in the combat effective zone with NO misses. Note where you lost control.

Drill 1:										Best Time
Times									
Key Notes:									

Drill 2:										Best Time
Times									
Key Notes:									

Drill 3:										Best Time
Times									
Key Notes:									

Competition Handgun Training Logbook

Drill 4:										Best Time
Key Notes:										
Key Notes:										

Success Analysis: (What I did really well)

_____
_____
_____
_____

Solution Analysis: (What I figured out or need to figure out)

_____
_____
_____
_____

General Notes: (Any additional notes on the training session)

_____
_____
_____
_____

Carry Over (write any **key notes** you want to stand out to you in your next training session on that future log page):

_____
_____
_____
_____

Competition Handgun Training Logbook

General Details

** DID YOU REVIEW YOUR LAST TRAINING LOG FOR KEY INFORMATION BEFORE BEGINNING?? **

Extra Session: _____ Date: _____ Weather: Sunny Cloudy Rain Snow Windy Temp: _____

Gun: _____ Problems? Yes - No   Ammo: _____ Problems? Yes - No

Mental Routine: Combat (focus) Breath? Yes – No   Active Visualization? Yes - No   Passive Visualization? Yes - No

---

*Record your average times, and your best times. Constantly strive to push harder, while maintaining control. Note your best time. On smaller drills record averages and best times, but recording every repetition is not necessary.
**Maintain a speed where you can hit 90% accuracy in the combat effective zone with NO misses. Note where you lost control.

Drill 1: | Best Time

Times										

Key Notes:

Drill 2: | Best Time

Times										

Key Notes:

Drill 3: | Best Time

Times										

Key Notes:

Copyright 2013, All rights reserved   www.shooting-performance.com

Competition Handgun Training Logbook

Drill 4:										Best Time
Key Notes:										
Key Notes:										

Success Analysis: (What I did really well)
_____
_____
_____
_____

Solution Analysis: (What I figured out or need to figure out)
_____
_____
_____
_____

General Notes: (Any additional notes on the training session)
_____
_____
_____
_____
_____

Carry Over (write any **key notes** you want to stand out to you in your next training session on that future log page):
_____
_____
_____
_____

Competition Handgun Training Logbook

General Details

** DID YOU REVIEW YOUR LAST TRAINING LOG FOR KEY INFORMATION BEFORE BEGINNING?? **

Extra Session: _____ Date: _____ Weather: Sunny Cloudy Rain Snow Windy Temp: _____

Gun: _____ Problems? Yes - No   Ammo: _____ Problems? Yes - No

Mental Routine: Combat (focus) Breath? Yes – No   Active Visualization? Yes - No   Passive Visualization? Yes - No

---

*Record your average times, and your best times. Constantly strive to push harder, while maintaining control. Note your best time. On smaller drills record averages and best times, but recording every repetition is not necessary.

**Maintain a speed where you can hit 90% accuracy in the combat effective zone with NO misses. Note where you lost control.

Drill 1:										**Best Time**
Times									
Key Notes:									

Drill 2:										**Best Time**
Times									
Key Notes:									

Drill 3:										**Best Time**
Times									
Key Notes:									

Copyright 2013, All rights reserved   www.shooting-performance.com

Competition Handgun Training Logbook

Drill 4:											Best Time
Key Notes:											
Key Notes:											

Success Analysis: (What I did really well)
_____
_____
_____
_____

Solution Analysis: (What I figured out or need to figure out)
_____
_____
_____
_____

General Notes: (Any additional notes on the training session)
_____
_____
_____
_____

Carry Over (write any **key notes** you want to stand out to you in your next training session on that future log page):
_____
_____
_____
_____

Competition Handgun Training Logbook

Match/Event Logs

"Treat every [game] as preparation for the next one"

Competition Handgun Training Logbook

Instructions: These Match/Event log sheets are general in design and will allow you to record your training sessions, and all critical and relevant information. You can either take your logbook to the match with you and log each stage as you shoot it, or take notes on your match booklet and transfer them later. Either way, make sure you take detailed notes at some point that will allow you to learn and make changes to your training program. Each section has a specific purpose, and here are some guidelines for each section:

- **General Details.** This section should be self-explanatory. It is formatted so you can quickly jot down the details that will be important to you later on. Circle the appropriate answers, or write in the details.
- **Performance Metrics.** This section starts with a table that will allow you to log the stage details (for 10 stages) in one area, for quick review later. The table includes:
    - *Stage*: write the stage number or name down here.
    - *Time*: Write your time here, if N/A, write that.
    - *Points*: Write your stage points here.
    - *Penalties*: Write your total penalties here.
    - *Hit Factor*: Figure out the hit factor or final score (IPDA) for the stage after penalties.
    - *%/Finish*: Write down your finish and % of the stage winners here.
- **Stage Analysis:** These sections will allow you to write some more details down for each stage, and includes the following:
    - *Stage*: List the stage name.
    - *Finish*: List your overall finish on that stage.
    - *Time*: This is self-explanatory.
    - *Points*: This is self-explanatory.
    - *Penalties*: List your total penalties here (you can list # of penalties, or total points, whatever your preference).
    - *Control Zone*: I break down control zones and circle what zone I shot the stage in. Zone 1 is a speed zone where I am shooting very slow and controlled, and so much so that I am giving away time. When in zone 1, I am in control, but have more control than I need. Zone 2 is where I want to be when I am at a practical type match, and it is a zone where speed and points are both equally relevant yet I am in control and feel that way. Zone 3 is the redline zone, and is a zone that we

should rarely if ever be in. If I am deliberately in zone 3, it is a match situation where I need it to try to win, and have accepted the potential risk.
  - *Key Notes*: Write the key details about what happened to you on the stage here. Keep it short and relevant for future use in training program modification, or match preparation.
- **Training Program addition/modification:** This section will be used to document needs in your training program, such as skills or areas that you were not comfortable with during the event. This is what you will reflect upon before your next training session. Make sure to transfer this information to your next training log, as a reminder to modify or add a drill to build whatever skill you were lacking in.
- **Success Analysis:** This section will give you a chance to reinforce positive actions and performances. Take some time to list all of the things your did really well, and why you did them well here.
- **Gear:** Use this section to critique your gear and how it performed (or failed to!). Ammunition power factor (if they chronoed at the match), as well as other key details about how your ammunition performed is also a good thing to note, for future reference.

Competition Handgun Training Logbook

General Details

Event: _____ Date: _____ Weather: Sunny Cloudy Rain Snow Windy Temp: _____

Gun: _____ Problems: Y N Ammo: _____ Holster/Rig: IPSC - IDPA – Carry

Video Taken: Y N   Emotional Control Zone (overall): 1 - 2 - 3   Did Active Visualization? Yes - No

Today I felt: Great Good Mediocre Sick   Overall Finish: _____ Accuracy %: _____ Penalties: _____

GM/Professionals at match (to help track my finish against them):
_____

Performance Metrics

Training Program addition/modification (drills I need to add or modify based on analysis above):
_____
_____
_____
_____

Success Analysis (What I did really well, I can minimize training in these areas):
_____
_____
_____
_____
_____
_____

Gear (How my gear did):
_____
_____
_____
_____
_____
_____
_____

Competition Handgun Training Logbook

Stages

Stage 1	Time:	Points:	Penalties:	Plan: Y N Visualize: Y N Execute Plan: Y N
Analysis (why did you succeed or fall short of your own potential on this stage):				

Stage 2	Time:	Points:	Penalties:	Plan: Y N Visualize: Y N Execute Plan: Y N
Analysis (why did you succeed or fall short of your own potential on this stage):				

Stage 3	Time:	Points:	Penalties:	Plan: Y N Visualize: Y N Execute Plan: Y N
Analysis (why did you succeed or fall short of your own potential on this stage):				

Stage 4	Time:	Points:	Penalties:	Plan: Y N Visualize: Y N Execute Plan: Y N
Analysis (why did you succeed or fall short of your own potential on this stage):				

Stage 5	Time:	Points:	Penalties:	Plan: Y N Visualize: Y N Execute Plan: Y N
Analysis (why did you succeed or fall short of your own potential on this stage):				

Stage 6	Time:	Points:	Penalties:	Plan: Y N Visualize: Y N Execute Plan: Y N
Analysis (why did you succeed or fall short of your own potential on this stage):				

Stage 7	Time:	Points:	Penalties:	Plan: Y N Visualize: Y N Execute Plan: Y N
Analysis (why did you succeed or fall short of your own potential on this stage):				

Stage 8	Time:	Points:	Penalties:	Plan: Y N Visualize: Y N Execute Plan: Y N
Analysis (why did you succeed or fall short of your own potential on this stage):				

Competition Handgun Training Logbook

General Details

Event: _____ Date: _____ Weather: Sunny Cloudy Rain Snow Windy Temp: _____

Gun: _____ Problems: Y N Ammo: _____ Holster/Rig: IPSC - IDPA – Carry

Video Taken: Y N   Emotional Control Zone (overall): 1 - 2 - 3   Did Active Visualization? Yes - No

Today I felt: Great Good Mediocre Sick   Overall Finish: _____   Accuracy %: _____   Penalties: _____

GM/Professionals at match (to help track my finish against them):
_____

Performance Metrics

Training Program addition/modification (drills I need to add or modify based on analysis above):

_____
_____
_____
_____

Success Analysis (What I did really well, I can minimize training in these areas):

_____
_____
_____
_____
_____
_____

Gear (How my gear did):

_____
_____
_____
_____
_____
_____
_____

Competition Handgun Training Logbook

Stages

Stage 1	Time:	Points:	Penalties:	Plan: Y N Visualize: Y N Execute Plan: Y N
Analysis (why did you succeed or fall short of your own potential on this stage):				

Stage 2	Time:	Points:	Penalties:	Plan: Y N Visualize: Y N Execute Plan: Y N
Analysis (why did you succeed or fall short of your own potential on this stage):				

Stage 3	Time:	Points:	Penalties:	Plan: Y N Visualize: Y N Execute Plan: Y N
Analysis (why did you succeed or fall short of your own potential on this stage):				

Stage 4	Time:	Points:	Penalties:	Plan: Y N Visualize: Y N Execute Plan: Y N
Analysis (why did you succeed or fall short of your own potential on this stage):				

Stage 5	Time:	Points:	Penalties:	Plan: Y N Visualize: Y N Execute Plan: Y N
Analysis (why did you succeed or fall short of your own potential on this stage):				

Stage 6	Time:	Points:	Penalties:	Plan: Y N Visualize: Y N Execute Plan: Y N
Analysis (why did you succeed or fall short of your own potential on this stage):				

Stage 7	Time:	Points:	Penalties:	Plan: Y N Visualize: Y N Execute Plan: Y N
Analysis (why did you succeed or fall short of your own potential on this stage):				

Stage 8	Time:	Points:	Penalties:	Plan: Y N Visualize: Y N Execute Plan: Y N
Analysis (why did you succeed or fall short of your own potential on this stage):				

Competition Handgun Training Logbook

General Details

Event: _____ Date: _____ Weather: Sunny Cloudy Rain Snow Windy Temp: _____

Gun: _____ Problems: Y N   Ammo: _____ Holster/Rig: IPSC - IDPA – Carry

Video Taken: Y N   Emotional Control Zone (overall): 1 - 2 - 3   Did Active Visualization? Yes - No

Today I felt: Great Good Mediocre Sick   Overall Finish: _____   Accuracy %: _____   Penalties: _____

GM/Professionals at match (to help track my finish against them):
_____

Performance Metrics

Training Program addition/modification (drills I need to add or modify based on analysis above):
_____
_____
_____
_____

Success Analysis (What I did really well, I can minimize training in these areas):
_____
_____
_____
_____
_____

Gear (How my gear did):
_____
_____
_____
_____
_____
_____

Competition Handgun Training Logbook

Stages

Stage 1	Time:	Points:	Penalties:	Plan: Y N Visualize: Y N Execute Plan: Y N
Analysis (why did you succeed or fall short of your own potential on this stage):				

Stage 2	Time:	Points:	Penalties:	Plan: Y N Visualize: Y N Execute Plan: Y N
Analysis (why did you succeed or fall short of your own potential on this stage):				

Stage 3	Time:	Points:	Penalties:	Plan: Y N Visualize: Y N Execute Plan: Y N
Analysis (why did you succeed or fall short of your own potential on this stage):				

Stage 4	Time:	Points:	Penalties:	Plan: Y N Visualize: Y N Execute Plan: Y N
Analysis (why did you succeed or fall short of your own potential on this stage):				

Stage 5	Time:	Points:	Penalties:	Plan: Y N Visualize: Y N Execute Plan: Y N
Analysis (why did you succeed or fall short of your own potential on this stage):				

Stage 6	Time:	Points:	Penalties:	Plan: Y N Visualize: Y N Execute Plan: Y N
Analysis (why did you succeed or fall short of your own potential on this stage):				

Stage 7	Time:	Points:	Penalties:	Plan: Y N Visualize: Y N Execute Plan: Y N
Analysis (why did you succeed or fall short of your own potential on this stage):				

Stage 8	Time:	Points:	Penalties:	Plan: Y N Visualize: Y N Execute Plan: Y N
Analysis (why did you succeed or fall short of your own potential on this stage):				

Competition Handgun Training Logbook

General Details

Event: _____ Date: _____ Weather: Sunny Cloudy Rain Snow Windy Temp: _____

Gun: _____ Problems: Y N Ammo: _____ Holster/Rig: IPSC - IDPA – Carry

Video Taken: Y N   Emotional Control Zone (overall): 1 - 2 - 3   Did Active Visualization? Yes - No

Today I felt: Great Good Mediocre Sick   Overall Finish: _____   Accuracy %: _____   Penalties: _____

GM/Professionals at match (to help track my finish against them):
_____

Performance Metrics

Training Program addition/modification (drills I need to add or modify based on analysis above):
_____
_____
_____

Success Analysis (What I did really well, I can minimize training in these areas):
_____
_____
_____
_____
_____

Gear (How my gear did):
_____
_____
_____
_____
_____
_____

Competition Handgun Training Logbook

Stages

Stage 1	Time:	Points:	Penalties:	Plan: Y N Visualize: Y N Execute Plan: Y N
Analysis (why did you succeed or fall short of your own potential on this stage):			

Stage 2	Time:	Points:	Penalties:	Plan: Y N Visualize: Y N Execute Plan: Y N
Analysis (why did you succeed or fall short of your own potential on this stage):			

Stage 3	Time:	Points:	Penalties:	Plan: Y N Visualize: Y N Execute Plan: Y N
Analysis (why did you succeed or fall short of your own potential on this stage):			

Stage 4	Time:	Points:	Penalties:	Plan: Y N Visualize: Y N Execute Plan: Y N
Analysis (why did you succeed or fall short of your own potential on this stage):			

Stage 5	Time:	Points:	Penalties:	Plan: Y N Visualize: Y N Execute Plan: Y N
Analysis (why did you succeed or fall short of your own potential on this stage):			

Stage 6	Time:	Points:	Penalties:	Plan: Y N Visualize: Y N Execute Plan: Y N
Analysis (why did you succeed or fall short of your own potential on this stage):			

Stage 7	Time:	Points:	Penalties:	Plan: Y N Visualize: Y N Execute Plan: Y N
Analysis (why did you succeed or fall short of your own potential on this stage):			

Stage 8	Time:	Points:	Penalties:	Plan: Y N Visualize: Y N Execute Plan: Y N
Analysis (why did you succeed or fall short of your own potential on this stage):			

Copyright 2013, All rights reserved

www.shooting-performance.com

Competition Handgun Training Logbook

General Details

Event: _____ Date: _____ Weather: Sunny Cloudy Rain Snow Windy Temp: _____

Gun: _____ Problems: Y N Ammo: _____ Holster/Rig: IPSC - IDPA – Carry

Video Taken: Y N   Emotional Control Zone (overall): 1 - 2 - 3   Did Active Visualization? Yes - No

Today I felt: Great Good Mediocre Sick   Overall Finish: _____   Accuracy %: _____   Penalties: _____

GM/Professionals at match (to help track my finish against them):
_____

Performance Metrics

Training Program addition/modification (drills I need to add or modify based on analysis above):
_____
_____
_____
_____

Success Analysis (What I did really well, I can minimize training in these areas):
_____
_____
_____
_____
_____
_____

Gear (How my gear did):
_____
_____
_____
_____
_____
_____
_____

Competition Handgun Training Logbook

Stages

Stage 1	Time:	Points:	Penalties:	Plan: Y N Visualize: Y N Execute Plan: Y N
Analysis (why did you succeed or fall short of your own potential on this stage):					

Stage 2	Time:	Points:	Penalties:	Plan: Y N Visualize: Y N Execute Plan: Y N
Analysis (why did you succeed or fall short of your own potential on this stage):					

Stage 3	Time:	Points:	Penalties:	Plan: Y N Visualize: Y N Execute Plan: Y N
Analysis (why did you succeed or fall short of your own potential on this stage):					

Stage 4	Time:	Points:	Penalties:	Plan: Y N Visualize: Y N Execute Plan: Y N
Analysis (why did you succeed or fall short of your own potential on this stage):					

Stage 5	Time:	Points:	Penalties:	Plan: Y N Visualize: Y N Execute Plan: Y N
Analysis (why did you succeed or fall short of your own potential on this stage):					

Stage 6	Time:	Points:	Penalties:	Plan: Y N Visualize: Y N Execute Plan: Y N
Analysis (why did you succeed or fall short of your own potential on this stage):					

Stage 7	Time:	Points:	Penalties:	Plan: Y N Visualize: Y N Execute Plan: Y N
Analysis (why did you succeed or fall short of your own potential on this stage):					

Stage 8	Time:	Points:	Penalties:	Plan: Y N Visualize: Y N Execute Plan: Y N
Analysis (why did you succeed or fall short of your own potential on this stage):					

Copyright 2013, All rights reserved

www.shooting-performance.com

Skills Tests

Competition Handgun Training Logbook

Skills Test

Instructions: This skills test will be a base test that will allow you to test your marksmanship and manipulation skills at the current time. It will be invaluable when you want to see how much you are improving in the future, as well as for use on stages requiring you to know your times for one reason or another (like a stage with a swinger that you are trying to figure out how many static targets you can engage before you get back to the swinger).

There are two complete skills tests below, one to start with, and one to record times as you get through one of your many training cycles. I recommend the second one be shot at the end of the season, so you can compare times and see your improvement.

Test One

General Data

Date: _____

Name (only first name is required): _____

☐ USPSA or ☐ IDPA division (check one)

Current Classification Level/s: (please list all classifications)

USPSA- ☐ GM ☐ M ☐ A ☐ B ☐ C ☐ D ☐ UN

or

IDPA- ☐ MA ☐ EX ☐ SS ☐ MM ☐ UN

Division/s shot during this test (what gear you used)

USPSA- ☐ Limited ☐ Production ☐ Open ☐ Limited -10 ☐ Single Stack ☐ Revolver

IDPA- ☐ CDP ☐ ESP ☐ SSP ☐ SSR ☐ ESR ☐ BUG

Physical Limitations: _____

Firearm Model/Type (in the test): _____ Caliber: _____

Holster and Magazine Pouch type: _____

Ammunition ☐ Factory ☐ Hand loaded

Estimated Power Factor: _____

Skills

Skill: STATIONARY DRAW

Target: IPSC Standard set 5 feet high at the shoulder

Distance: 5, 7, 10, 15, and 25 yards

Start Position: Hands relaxed at sides and surrender position

Skill Details: Draw and fire one shot, and record time. Repeat five times at each distance and record the average time on an unflawed draw by totaling the time and dividing by 5.

Notes: Hits must be done at a speed that is controlled, hits must be A/C's. Perform the skill test at a speed that guarantees an A/C hit.

Times:	1	2	3	4	5	Total	/5 = average
5							
7							
10							
15							
25							
Surrender draw							
5							
7							
10							
15							
25							

Competition Handgun Training Logbook

Skill: 90 AND 180-DEGREE TURN AND DRAW

Target: IPSC Standard set 5 feet high at the shoulder

Distance: 10 yards

Start Position: Hands relaxed at sides facing left, right, or uprange.

Skill Details: Record times for the 90 and 180 degree pivot at 5-25 yards. Upon sound of the pact timer, turn and fire one shot, record time. Repeat 5 times for the 90 and 180 turns.

Notes: We will test the 90-degree pivot with the gun side facing the target, and the 180 pivots in the direction you choose to go (fastest).

Times:	1	2	3	4	5	Total	/5 = average
90 degree							
180 degree							

Skill: WEAK HAND DRAW AND TRANSFER

Target: IPSC Standard set 5 feet high at the shoulder

Distance: 10 yards

Start Position: Hands relaxed at sides

Skill Details: Draw, transfer to the weak hand and fire one shot, and record time. Repeat 5 times and make up flawed draws. Record and average 5 times.

Notes: Please skip this test if you do not know how to safely transfer the gun.

Times:	1	2	3	4	5	Total	/5 = average

Competition Handgun Training Logbook

Skill: RELOAD

Target: IPSC Standard set 5 feet high at the shoulder

Distance: 10 yards

Start Position: Hands relaxed at sides

Skill Details: Draw and fire one shot, reload, and fire one shot. Record the split (reload) time. Repeat and record 5 times and average.

Notes: This drill we will measure the speed reload. If you are an IDPA shooter, then test the slidelock reload.

Times:	1	2	3	4	5	Total	/5 = average

Skill: RECOIL CONTROL (SPLIT TIMES BETWEEN SHOTS)

Target: IPSC Standard set 5 feet high at the shoulder

Distance: 5, 7, 10, 15, and 25 yards

Start Position: Hands relaxed at sides

Skill Details: Draw and fire two shots, and record the slit time. Record 5 times for each distance.

Notes: Hits must be done at a speed that is controlled, hits must be A/C's. Perform the skill test at a speed that guarantees an A/C hit.

Times:	1	2	3	4	5	Total	/5 = average
5							
7							
10							
15							
25							

Competition Handgun Training Logbook

Skill: TARGET AQUISITION

Target: 2 IPSC Standard targets set 5 feet high at the shoulder. Target should have the following distances between them: 1 Yard, 3 yards, 5 yards, 10 Yards

Distance: 5 and 10 yards

Start Position: Hands relaxed at sides

Skill Details: Draw and fire one shot on the left target, and one on the right target. Record the split time (time transitioning the gun to the next target).

Notes: Record times for targets 1, 3, 5, and 10 yards apart at 5 yards, then at 10 yards.

Yards between targets	Repetitions					Total	/5 = average
Distance: 5 yards							
1							
3							
5							
10							
Distance: 10 yards							
1							
3							
5							
10							

Skill: 6 SHOT DRILL (BILL DRILL)

Target: IPSC Standard set 5 feet high at the shoulder

Distance: 10 yards

Start Position: Hands relaxed at sides

Skill Details: Draw and fire six shots, and record the total time. Record and average 5 times.

Notes: Hits must be done at a speed that is controlled, hits must be A/C's. Perform the skill test at a speed that guarantees an A/C hit.

Times:	1	2	3	4	5	Total	/5 = average

Skill: EL PRESIDENTE

Target: 3 IPSC Standard set 5 feet high at the shoulder, one yard apart

Distance: 10 yards

Start Position: Wrists above shoulders, facing up range (away from targets)

Skill Details: Turn, draw and fire six shots (two on each target), reload, and fire six shots (two on each target), and record the total time. Record and average 5 times.

Notes: Hits must be done at a speed that is controlled, hits must be A/C's. Perform the skill test at a speed that guarantees an A/C hit.

Times:	1	2	3	4	5	Total	/5 = average

Competition Handgun Training Logbook

Test Two

General Data

Date: _____

Name (only first name is required): _____

☐ USPSA or ☐ IDPA division (check one)

Current Classification Level/s: (please list all classifications)

USPSA- ☐ GM ☐ M ☐ A ☐ B ☐ C ☐ D ☐ UN

or

IDPA- ☐ MA ☐ EX ☐ SS ☐ MM ☐ UN

Division/s shot during this test (what gear you used)

USPSA- ☐ Limited ☐ Production ☐ Open ☐ Limited -10 ☐ Single Stack ☐ Revolver

IDPA- ☐ CDP ☐ ESP ☐ SSP ☐ SSR ☐ ESR ☐ BUG

Physical Limitations: _____

Firearm Model/Type (in the test): _____ Caliber: _____

Holster and Magazine Pouch type: _____

Ammunition ☐ Factory ☐ Hand loaded

Estimated Power Factor: _____

Skills

Skill: STATIONARY DRAW

Target: IPSC Standard set 5 feet high at the shoulder

Distance: 5, 7, 10, 15, and 25 yards

Start Position: Hands relaxed at sides and surrender position

Skill Details: Draw and fire one shot, and record time. Repeat five times at each distance and record the average time on an unflawed draw by totaling the time and dividing by 5.

Notes: Hits must be done at a speed that is controlled, hits must be A/C's. Perform the skill test at a speed that guarantees an A/C hit.

Times:	1	2	3	4	5	Total	/5 = average
5							
7							
10							
15							
25							
Surrender draw							
5							
7							
10							
15							
25							

Competition Handgun Training Logbook

Skill: 90 AND 180-DEGREE TURN AND DRAW

Target: IPSC Standard set 5 feet high at the shoulder

Distance: 10 yards

Start Position: Hands relaxed at sides facing left, right, or uprange.

Skill Details: Record times for the 90 and 180 degree pivot at 5-25 yards. Upon sound of the pact timer, turn and fire one shot, record time. Repeat 5 times for the 90 and 180 turns.

Notes: We will test the 90-degree pivot with the gun side facing the target, and the 180 pivots in the direction you choose to go (fastest).

Times:	1	2	3	4	5	Total	/5 = average
90 degree							
180 degree							

Skill: WEAK HAND DRAW AND TRANSFER

Target: IPSC Standard set 5 feet high at the shoulder

Distance: 10 yards

Start Position: Hands relaxed at sides

Skill Details: Draw, transfer to the weak hand and fire one shot, and record time. Repeat 5 times and make up flawed draws. Record and average 5 times.

Notes: Please skip this test if you do not know how to safely transfer the gun.

Times:	1	2	3	4	5	Total	/5 = average

Competition Handgun Training Logbook

Skill: RELOAD

Target: IPSC Standard set 5 feet high at the shoulder

Distance: 10 yards

Start Position: Hands relaxed at sides

Skill Details: Draw and fire one shot, reload, and fire one shot. Record the split (reload) time. Repeat and record 5 times and average.

Notes: This drill we will measure the speed reload. If you are an IDPA shooter, then test the slidelock reload.

Times:	1	2	3	4	5	Total	/5 = average

Skill: RECOIL CONTROL (SPLIT TIMES BETWEEN SHOTS)

Target: IPSC Standard set 5 feet high at the shoulder

Distance: 5, 7, 10, 15, and 25 yards

Start Position: Hands relaxed at sides

Skill Details: Draw and fire two shots, and record the slit time. Record 5 times for each distance.

Notes: Hits must be done at a speed that is controlled, hits must be A/C's. Perform the skill test at a speed that guarantees an A/C hit.

Times:	1	2	3	4	5	Total	/5 = average
5							
7							
10							
15							
25							

Competition Handgun Training Logbook

Skill: TARGET AQUISITION

Target: 2 IPSC Standard targets set 5 feet high at the shoulder. Target should have the following distances between them: 1 Yard, 3 yards, 5 yards, 10 Yards

Distance: 5 and 10 yards

Start Position: Hands relaxed at sides

Skill Details: Draw and fire one shot on the left target, and one on the right target. Record the split time (time transitioning the gun to the next target).

Notes: Record times for targets 1, 3, 5, and 10 yards apart at 5 yards, then at 10 yards.

Yards between targets	Repetitions					Total	/5 = average
Distance: 5 yards							
1							
3							
5							
10							
Distance: 10 yards							
1							
3							
5							
10							

Skill: 6 SHOT DRILL (BILL DRILL)

Target: IPSC Standard set 5 feet high at the shoulder

Distance: 10 yards

Start Position: Hands relaxed at sides

Skill Details: Draw and fire six shots, and record the total time. Record and average 5 times.

Notes: Hits must be done at a speed that is controlled, hits must be A/C's. Perform the skill test at a speed that guarantees an A/C hit.

Times:	1	2	3	4	5	Total	/5 = average

Skill: EL PRESIDENTE

Target: 3 IPSC Standard set 5 feet high at the shoulder, one yard apart

Distance: 10 yards

Start Position: Wrists above shoulders, facing up range (away from targets)

Skill Details: Turn, draw and fire six shots (two on each target), reload, and fire six shots (two on each target), and record the total time. Record and average 5 times.

Notes: Hits must be done at a speed that is controlled, hits must be A/C's. Perform the skill test at a speed that guarantees an A/C hit.

Times:	1	2	3	4	5	Total	/5 = average

More about Shooting-Performance, (www.shooting-performance.com):

Founded in 2007, Shooting-Performance is a training, consulting, and research company that specializes in performance related firearm instruction and information for use in both combative and competitive environments. Mike Seeklander, owner/founder has extensive experience in and has been a full time instructor since December of 2001. For more information, please visit www.shooting-performance.com.

Thanks for your interest in Shooting-Performance, and taking the time to use this logbook.

Until Then, Train Hard!

Mike Seeklander

To order a copy of this book or other books and DVD's, please visit my website.